B 'Welcome to All', a lithograph of 1880 by Joseph Keppler, illustrating America's willingness to take in people who felt they had to leave their own countries.

Germany and the Scandinavian countries. Most of them were Protestants. Some of them were escaping poverty, others were escaping bad treatment because of their religious beliefs. Many had heard about the better life which was said to be waiting for them in the 'New World'. They weren't, of course, the only large religious or racial groups in the country. Since the 17th century large numbers of Negro slaves had been brought against their will into America from Africa. The native American peoples were also being treated badly.

A new age of immigration began in the second half of the 19th century. Large numbers of Irish Catholics went to America after the terrible potato famine of the 1840s. They were joined by Italians, Poles, Russians, Japanese and Chinese. The numbers continued to rise in the first two decades of the 20th century.

Changing attitudes towards immigrants

In 1882 an Act was passed which limited the number of Chinese immigrants as workers in California had been worried about losing their jobs to Chinese. During the First World War some Americans from central Europe weren't sure which side to support (the USA fought against Germany and Austria) – their 'new' country or the country they had been born in. These are just two of the reasons why attitudes towards immigrants gradually began to change.

A communist threat?

In 1917 a **communist** government took power in Russia. Some Americans feared that communism might spread to the USA. When the First World War ended in November 1918 there were economic problems. In January 1919 a number of factories which made weapons close[d] [and there was] more unemployment. In th[ere was] a communist uprising in Ge[rmany.] Americans suffered a rise in prices and, to make matters worse, in July 1919 there were violent clashes between blacks and whites in Chicago. The violence spread to 20 other cities – even the police went on strike in Boston!

Isolationism

The USA had stayed out of the First World War when it began in 1914. Many Americans were more keen to get on with their own lives and problems, rather than face death in faraway Europe. As the war went on, however, it became harder to remain neutral.

In 1915 a German U-boat sank the liner *Lusitania*. Among those drowned were 128 American passengers. In addition, American merchant ships were torpedoed by mistake by German U-boats and there were rumours that Germans were plotting to help Mexicans attack the USA.

Eventually in 1917 the USA entered the war against Germany. American money, equipment and soldiers helped defeat the Germans in 1918.

Suspicion of foreigners did not stop with the end of the First World War. Many Americans supported a policy of **isolationism**. They wanted the USA to stay out of wars and other problems in Europe and only concern themselves with things which mattered at home in the USA. President Wilson hated war and wanted to set up a new international body called the **League of Nations**. Its job would be to encourage the countries of the world to sort out their problems through discussion, rather than through fighting. The **Senate** refused to accept the Treaty of Versailles and the USA did not join the new League of Nations. Many Senators feared that if the USA got involved in peacemaking and became the world's policeman, then it might soon get dragged into another European war.

1 From which countries or parts of the world did people come to America? Make a list.
2 Why did people go to America?
3 Look at source A.
  a) Give the role of the following: President; and Congress.
  b) In what ways is the President very powerful?
  c) In what ways are the powers of the President limited?

THE 'RED SCARE' OF 1919

Anarchists?

When in August 1919 the house of America's chief law officer, Mitchell Palmer, was blown up, foreign **anarchists** were suspected of the crime. These people were not communists, but they alarmed many Americans because they were 'foreigners'. In place of Germany the new enemy seemed to be the foreign worker who had just arrived in the USA, who probably could not speak English, and who seemed to be out to take the American workers' jobs.

There is no evidence that these new immigrants were communist revolutionaries, but in hard times people began to panic and were ready to blame foreigners, blacks or other minorities for the USA's problems. Palmer was an ambitious man and thought that his warnings about communist revolution would make him popular.

The Palmer Raids

In August 1919 over four million workers went on strike. Most of the workers were not communists – they were striking for better wages and working conditions. Mitchell Palmer launched a series of raids in which 'foreign radicals' were arrested and kept in jail without trial. He set up a General Intelligence Division in the Department of Justice. It was run by J Edgar Hoover and spied on '**Reds**' and other supposedly dangerous people. In January 1920 Hoover's agents and local police organised raids on 'Reds' in 33 cities. A number of people were ordered to leave the USA.

For a while people put up with these raids. Palmer warned that anarchists and communists were planning huge terrorist demonstrations for May Day 1920. Thousands of police and special troops were put on standby. When the expected riots did not happen, people lost faith in Palmer and began to criticise the raids and their threat to ordinary people's freedom. The 'Red Scare' was over – and so were Palmer's chances of becoming President.

The quota system

In 1921 an Immigration Act was passed which allowed only about 350 000 immigrants to enter the USA each year. By 1929 this number had fallen to 150 000. A carefully organised **quota** system meant the American government could make sure that large numbers of people from 'undesirable' countries were kept out. Sources A and B give clues about those countries.

In May 1920 two Italian immigrants were arrested for being involved in a wages robbery. The bullets in their guns were of the same type as those used in the raid. Sacco and Vanzetti were anarchists and they spoke no English. Their lawyer said that they had been somewhere else when the robbery took place, but the jury found them guilty and they were sent to the electric chair. Many people believe they were innocent.

A 'Foreign-born population in the United States in 1920': an illustration based on a diagram printed in an American magazine in that year.

Germany 1 683 298
Italy 1 607 458
Russia 1 398 999
Poland 1 139 578
Great Britain 1 133 967
Canada 1 117 136
Ireland 1 035 680
Sweden 624 759
Austria 574 959
Mexico 476 676
Hungary 397 081
Norway 363 599
Denmark 189 051
Greece 175 701
France 152 792
Finland 149 671
Holland 131 262
Switzerland 118 647
Asia 110 586
Romania 103 007

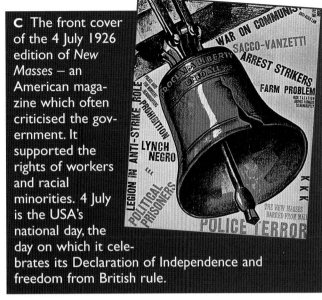

C The front cover of the 4 July 1926 edition of *New Masses* — an American magazine which often criticised the government. It supported the rights of workers and racial minorities. 4 July is the USA's national day, the day on which it celebrates its Declaration of Independence and freedom from British rule.

	Effects	
	1921	*1924*
Number of imigrants restricted to:	*3% of 1910 population*	*2% of 1890 population*
Europe		
UK/Ireland	77 342	62 574
Germany/Austria	75 510	52 012
Eastern Europe	63 191	10 902
Italy	42 957	3 845
Scandinavia	41 859	19 274
Russia	34 284	2 248
Rest of Europe	20 263	10 691
Asia	1 043	1 300
Africa	122	1 200
Rest of the world	424	621

B This table shows the numbers of immigrants allowed into the USA in 1921 and 1924 by the quota system. The 1921 policy allowed the numbers shown to enter from each of the countries or regions, eg 77 342 immigrants would be allowed into the USA from the UK and Ireland each year. But in 1924 the policy was changed to make it much harder for immigrants from *some* countries to enter the USA.

D Relatives of people arrested during the 'Red Scare' raids protest outside the White House.

1 Look at source B. Draw bar charts or graphs to show the numbers of immigrants allowed into the USA in:
   a) 1921; and
   b) 1924.
2 Make a timeline of events described in this unit and call it 'The Red Scare'.
3 Why do you think there was a 'Red Scare' in 1919?
4 Look at sources A and B, and the rest of this unit. What kind of people do you think the American government was trying to:
   a) encourage to come to the USA; and

b) discourage from coming to the USA?
5 Some people complained that the USA was not a free country in the 1920s. Using sources C and D, as well as the rest of the information in this unit, make a list of those complaints.
6 Use the index in this book to help you find out about the following problems mentioned in source C. Try to write a couple of sentences about each of the following:
   a) 'KKK';
   b) 'Lynch Negro';
   c) 'Prohibition'; and
   d) 'Farm Problem'.

Progress for Women?

Who were the flappers? What evidence is there that life was changing for American women in the 1920s? Did the changes bring real progress for women?

A restricted life?

In 1900 many American women were treated like second class citizens. They were not allowed to vote and took little part in politics. Even their clothes were very restricted, as you can see from source A.

Social life was limited – even for richer women. The magazine from which source A was taken included an article about student life at Wellesley College. It explained that there were few rules except for those 'which would naturally govern the actions of any well-bred girl. While at college she is required to have a chaperone [an older person] supervising her at any entertainment in Boston, or to a football game at Harvard, or to an afternoon tea, just as she would be if she were at home with her own people'.

It was thought to be unladylike to smoke or drink in public. Divorce was quite rare – only 81 out of every 1000 marriages ended in divorce. Sex before marriage was not approved of. 74 per cent of the college students questioned in a survey in 1900 had not had sex before marriage.

Most women did not go out to work. Men had the best jobs.

A Fashions for young ladies at Wellesley College, as seen on the cover of the May 1908 issue of *Scribner's* magazine.

Flappers

In the 1920s a number of American women – mainly middle-class and upper-class women in the Northern states – rebelled against this restricted life. They were known as **flappers**. They cut their hair short and wore different clothes from the type worn by their mothers. The changes in clothes can be seen in sources A and B.

Clothes weren't the only things which changed. There seemed to be a change in attitudes too. Flappers began to smoke and drink alcohol in public. They went out to speakeasies on their own – without chaperones. Advertisements showed women smoking and driving cars. Attitudes towards sex and marriage seemed to be changing.

The name 'flapper' came from the way in which fashionable young ladies allowed their galoshes (boots) to 'flap' around their ankles.

The novelist Scott Fitzgerald wrote a novel called *In This Side of Paradise* which described the lifestyle of the rich young flappers. He wrote about 'the great current American phenomenon, the "petting party"' and commented that, 'None of the Victorian mothers had any idea how casually their daughters were accustomed to be kissed.' In *Echoes of the Jazz Age* Fitzgerald wrote that: 'The parties were bigger, the pace was faster, the shows were broader, the buildings were higher, the morals were looser and the liquor was cheaper.'

B A fashion page from *Woman's Journal*, December, 1927, which illustrates the sort of clothes worn by flappers.

C Two women being escorted off the beach by a policewoman.

A survey in 1920 found that only 31 per cent of the college students questioned had not had sex before marriage. New laws made it easier for women to divorce their husbands. By 1928 the number of marriages ending in divorce had risen to 166 out of every 1000.

The authorities in the state of Utah were so worried about the new fashions that they considered jailing women who were 'inappropriately dressed'.

Entertainment

Women went out to baseball games to see the new superstars, such as 'Babe' Ruth. There was exciting entertainment at the new cinemas which had been built all over the country. Millions of people – rich and poor, young and old, men and women – flocked to see Hollywood films with stars like Charlie Chaplin and Rudolph Valentino. There were exciting career opportunities for Hollywood actresses. Gloria Swanson and Jean Harlow became famous Hollywood stars. Ordinary Americans read about the lives of their heroines in the gossip columns. Mary Pickford was so rich and successful that she joined two other stars in setting up their own film company.

D From an article in the *New York Times* in 1922, written by a flapper.

A flapper is shameless, selfish and honest but at the same time she thinks of these things as good. Why not? She takes a man's point of view as her mother never could. When she loses she is not afraid to admit defeat, whether it be a lover or $20 at an auction. She will never make you a hatband or knit you a necktie, but she'll drive you from the station on hot summer nights in her own sportscar. She'll put on trousers and go skiing with you or, if it happens to be summertime, go swimming. She'll dive as well as you, perhaps better. She'll dance as long as you care to and she'll take everything you say the way you mean it, not getting sore or hurt.

1 What 'crime' do you think the women in source C have committed?
2 Compare sources A and B. How big a change do you think there had been by the 1920s in clothing?
3 Apart from clothes, what other changes were there in the position of women in the 1920s?
4 Which parts of source D do you think went most against traditional views of women?
5 How useful are sources A and B for measuring changes in the position of women in the 1920s?

DID WOMEN REALLY BENEFIT?

Women voters

After a long campaign women gained the vote in 1920. The National Women's Party, led by Alice Paul, tried to get full equality for women under the law. Their Equal Rights Amendment failed, partly because other women's groups opposed it.

Women workers

During the First World War a number of women worked for the first time. Some of these jobs had previously been done by men. Even though women proved that they could do these jobs just as well as the men, many lost their jobs when the men returned from the war.

Two million more women were employed in 1930 than in 1920. This was, however, an increase of only one per cent. Women earned almost a third of all degrees by 1930, but only four per cent of the professors were women. Women still tended to work in the least skilled and lowest paid jobs and men were still paid more than women for doing the same job. Women did not get much help from the government and the police. In 1927, for example, women textile workers went on strike in Tennessee. Police broke the strike by arresting workers. The government often took the side of the bosses rather than the workers in a strike. The **Supreme Court** banned laws which set a minimum wage for women workers. Men were the managers and had the jobs with the best prospects.

There were new jobs for women, but they tended to be so-called 'women's jobs' such as librarians, teachers and nurses. Some women had better jobs – for example, office work was easier and less tiring than working as a servant.

	1900	1930
Professional and technical workers	8	14
Managers and officials	1	3
Clerical and sales workers	8	28
Skilled craftspeople	1	1
Workers and labourers	26	19
Domestic servants	29	18
Other service workers	7	10
Farmers	6	2

A This table shows the changes in the percentages of women workers, 1900–30.

Most women workers had low-paying jobs. The number of women doctors actually decreased. For the most part the professions were reserved for men, with women relegated to teaching and nursing.

Women had won the right to vote in 1920, but this had less impact than its supporters had hoped. Once achieved, it robbed women of a unifying cause. Men remained the main breadwinners, women cooked, cleaned and raised the children.

Advertisers sought out women as buyers of consumer products, but wives only bought products their husbands allowed them to buy. Despite the talk of the 'new woman', the flappers fell victim to the sex-role conditioning of their parents. Boys continued to play with guns and grew up to head their families, girls played with dolls and looked forward to careers as wives and mothers.

Women speculators

In the 1920s women began to speculate (gamble) on the Wall Street stock market. Secretaries, businesswomen and housewives all bought stocks and shares. In 1919 only two per cent of the Stock Exchange gamblers were women. By 1929 the figure had risen to 35 per cent.

Marriage and work

Magazines reminded women that they should marry and have children – and that their place was in the home. The *Ladies Home Journal* told women that: 'The creation and fulfilment of a successful home is a bit of craftsmanship that compares favourably with building a beautiful cathedral.' Most American women got married. The 1910 **census** found that only seven per cent of women aged between 65 and 69 were not married. Once women married they tended to give up work. Many of those who carried on working did so because they could not afford to give up work. Black women were particularly badly paid. 31 per cent of black wives in New York worked in 1930. The figure for white wives was only four per cent. Women factory workers faced difficult conditions. There weren't many women in professional jobs – such as lawyers and doctors. In 1920, 88 per cent of the women in these jobs were single.

American women in the 1920s were having fewer children and living longer than their mothers and grandmothers. In 1850 women were expected to live for about 40 years. Improvements in medicine and public health caused the figure to rise to 51 by 1900 and to 63 by 1925. In 1900 American women had, on average, 3.6 children. This figure had fallen to 2.5 by 1930, but it didn't mean that women went back to work once the children had grown up.

E The young women in this photograph show several features of the 'flappers'. They are wearing short skirts, have short haircuts and are dancing the Charleston. The Charleston was a popular dance of the 1920s. It was very different from the old ballroom dancing and waltzes of America before the war.

C A farmer and his wife, pictured with their children. They have been forced to leave their farm. In the 1920s many American farmers were ruined when prices for their goods fell and they could no longer afford to stay on the land (page 34). About six million people left the countryside to look for work in cities. Some of them did not succeed.

D This table shows the changes in the typical items available for a family to buy in 1900 and 1928 (from an article in *Survey* magazine by Eunice Fuller Barnard, 1928).

1900	
Two bicycles	$70
Wringer and washboard	$5
Brushes and brooms	$5
Sewing machine (mechanical)	$25
Total	$105
1928	
Automobile	$700
Radio	$75
Record player	$50
Washing machine	$150
Vacuum cleaner	$50
Sewing machine (electric)	$60
Other electrical equipment	$25
Telephone	$35
Total	$1145

Q

1 What do the figures in source A tell you about the changes in women's work from 1900 to 1930?
2 How far did the position of women improve in the 1920s? Copy the chart and complete it with as many examples as you can find for both columns. Some suggestions have been put in as a guide.

Improvements	Things which stayed the same
Women got the vote	The Equal Rights Amendment failed
More women had worked in the war	Men got their jobs back after the war

3 How might the changes shown in source D have benefited women? Give as many examples as you can.
4 How far is it possible to use the figures in source A to support the views put forward in source B about changes in women's work? Give examples from both sources in your answer.
5 Look back over the information and evidence in this unit and explain whether you agree or disagree with this statement: 'The 1920s were a period of progress for American women.'

Black Americans

Slavery

In 1619 a Dutch ship arrived in Chesapeake Bay on the eastern coast of America with 20 'Negars' for sale. These are thought to have been the first black people in America. They worked as servants in the homes of white settlers in Jamestown, Virginia. By the 1660s laws had been passed in Virginia, Maryland and Massachusetts which allowed white people to keep black slaves.

The slaves were supplied by merchants from Britain and other European countries who traded in slaves from West Africa. It is estimated that 15 million people were transported across the Atlantic during the following two centuries.

'Jim Crow' laws

Some states tried to keep control over black people by passing '**Jim Crow**' **laws** to keep them separate or segregated from white people. This involved making sure that black people went to separate schools. Despite the fact that in 1862 President Lincoln freed the slaves, black people were still kept in poorly paid, unskilled jobs with few trade union rights. After the Civil War black people began to move to the cities in search of a better life. By 1910 the black population of New York had risen to 91 709. 30 years later it was 458 000.

In the First World War 360 000 black people served in the armed forces. They returned home to find that racism was still a part of everyday life. Many other blacks moved to the cities to work in the factories. In 1919 at least 70 black people were **lynched** and there were race riots in both Northern and Southern cities. New Jim Crow laws were passed in Southern states – so that there were segregated taxis, race tracks and boxing matches.

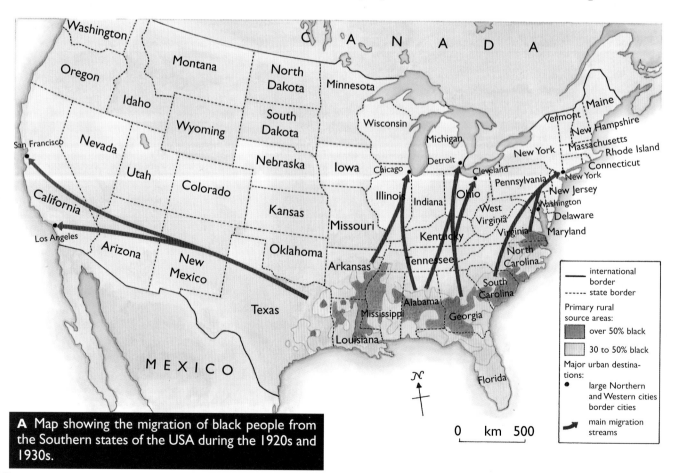

A Map showing the migration of black people from the Southern states of the USA during the 1920s and 1930s.

B A segregated drinking fountain.

C An article published in a black American newspaper in 1921 describes some of the reasons why black people left the Southern states.

Look around at your cabin, look at the dirt floor and the windows without glass. Then ask your folks already up North about the bathrooms with hot and cold water … the steam heat and the glistening hardwood floors which down home you only see when you polish them … What chance has the average black to get these things down home? And if he does get them how can he be sure that some night some poor white man will get his gang together and come round and drive him out? … Step on a train and ride for a day and night to freedom. Your nickel is worth as much as the other fellow's nickel in the Northern streetcars and you sit wherever you can find a seat. You tip your hat to no man unless you want to do so.

Q

1 Look at the map in source A.
  a) In which Southern states did most blacks live?
  b) List seven cities to which black Americans went when they left the south.
2 Read the sources and other information in this unit. Make a list of ways in which black people were discriminated against.
3 a) What do you think the photographer of source B was trying to 'say' about conditions for black people in the Southern states?
  b) What questions would you want to ask about the person who took the photograph used in source B to help you decide how useful it is as evidence to the historian of black people in the USA?
4 Using source C and the other evidence, explain why so many black people left the Southern states in the 1920s.

LYNCHING

Lynch mobs took the law into their own hands and got away with murder. In 1933 28 lynchings were reported. It is not known how many went unreported. The story of the death of George Arnwood may give you an idea of what lynching was all about.

In October 1933 a 22-year-old mentally handicapped black man called George Arnwood was arrested by police for allegedly assaulting an 82-year-old white woman. White townspeople announced that they were going to lynch George Arnwood even though he had not been charged with any crime.

Men pulled up a telegraph pole and used it as a battering ram to break down the door of the jail. They got the keys to his cell and beat George Arnwood to death. His body was dragged out of the jail by a mob of about 400 white people and strung up on a tree. Police stood and watched as the mob then cut down the body and dragged it through the town before finally setting it on fire. The dead man's ears and penis were cut off by the lynch mob.

Nobody was punished for the murder of George Arnwood. His story was not unique. In the Southern state of Georgia, for example, the lynching of another black man was followed by the burning of his body. Hundreds of white men and women, both old and young, danced around the fire while the black man burned. That same evening a dance was held in a nearby barn. White people came from far and wide to the celebration. Many were members of the Ku Klux Klan.

B A black man who was growing up in the 1920s remembers the lynch mobs of the 1920s and 1930s:

The lesson of the lynching was very clear to us – that you, as a black person, have a certain position, and that you'd better maintain that position because if you get out of it, this is the punishment. It's not a question of justice or right or wrong or law, this is something that we have the right to do and we will do it … We also knew that the sheriff and some of his policemen were also members of the Ku Klux Klan. It was open intimidation, part of the political process. There were few people in the white community who raised any objections to it. We knew that it was a total waste of time to go to the law to get protection against lynching.

A The lynching of a black American.

C Michael Mitchell remembers how his father, the black reporter Clarence Mitchell, was allowed to write a report about the lynching of George Arnwood:

My father said that they wanted him to interview people because they figured that a black reporter would really let blacks know what would happen to them if they got out of line. He began to talk with whites and he saw a young white mother bringing her child who was no more than seven or eight years old to see the charred body of the lynched man. The mother said 'look how we barbecued that nigger'.

Who were the Ku Klux Klan?

Between 1920 and 1925 about five million Americans are thought to have joined the Ku Klux Klan. Its members could be found in different parts of the USA – but particularly in the old 'slave states' of the South. Klansmen often met in secret at night, but they also paraded in broad daylight.

D 'This is her first lynching', a cartoon by Reginald Marsh in *The New Yorker*, September 1934.

Its members dressed in white sheets and wore white hoods. They carried American flags and lit burning crosses at their night-time meetings.

The leader of the Klan was a dentist called Hiram Evans. He called himself the Imperial Wizard. The officers of the Klan called themselves Klaliffs, Klokards, Kludds, Kligrapps and Klabees.

We have seen that they carried out lynchings of black people, but they also beat up and mutilated anyone they considered to be their enemy. They stripped some of their victims and put tar and feathers on their bodies. In July 1921 Chris Lochas, an American restaurant owner was 'run out' of the town of Pensacola, Florida, by police who were also secret members of the Ku Klux Klan. His 'crime' was being a 'foreigner' – he had Greek parents.

E Part of the rule book of the Ku Klux Klan gives us clues about its aims:

1 Is the motive prompting you to be a Klansman serious and unselfish?
2 Are you a native-born, white, non-Jewish American?
3 Are you absolutely opposed to and free of any allegiance of any nature to any cause, government, people, sect or ruler that is foreign to the United States of America?
4 Do you believe in the Christian religion?
5 Do you believe in and will you faithfully strive for the eternal maintenance of white supremacy?

1 Look at sources A, B and C. What can you learn from these sources about the attitudes of some whites towards black people?
2 Read sources B and C. Why do you think the whites involved in lynchings were so open about their activities? Back up your answer with evidence.
3 a) What do you think the person who drew the cartoon in source D was trying to 'say' about lynchings?
   b) The New Yorker is a Northern magazine. Do you think a Southern one would have published it? Explain your answer.
4 Read source E and then find out about the ideas of the Nazis. How much similarity do you think there is between the ideas of the Nazis and those of the Ku Klux Klan?

WHY DID PEOPLE JOIN THE KLAN?

People who hated Jews were attracted to the Ku Klux Klan because the Klan considered the Jews to be a dangerous, 'inferior' race. The Klan blamed Jews for many of America's problems. People who hated Catholics also joined the Klan because it claimed that it was protecting America's Protestant people against the 'danger' of the Catholic church. Some of the founding fathers of America had been Protestants who came to America to escape Catholic persecution.

People who were suspicious of communists were also attracted to the Klan. It claimed to stand for the traditional American **capitalist** way of life – against the threat of international communism. The Klan slogan was 'Native, white, Protestant supremacy'. These ideas were popular in the years following the Russian Revolution of 1917 and the 'Red Scare' (pages 4–5). Hiram Evans said that the Klan was fighting against 'aliens who are constantly trying to change our civilisation into something that will suit themselves better'.

The Ku Klux Klan had friends in high places. J K Vardaman, for example, was **Governor** of the state of Mississippi, which had a large black population. He made no secret of his racist views. In a speech to Congress in February 1914 Vardaman explained that he thought God had never intended that blacks and whites should live together on equal terms. He thought that the white people should rule, and that black people should not be allowed to vote. He blamed black people's laziness for the economic problems facing the South.

Ordinary shopkeepers joined the Klan because they feared that they might lose business from Klan members if they refused to put up the TWK sign (Trade With Klansmen).

The fall of the Klan

In 1921 a new Immigration law was passed (page 4). This made it harder for the Klan to claim that the government was not doing enough to control immigration.

The reputation of the Klan was damaged by a scandal involving the Indiana Klan leader, the 'Grand Dragon' David Stevenson. He was convicted of kidnapping, raping and murdering a young secretary.

In January 1923 a white woman claimed she had been robbed by a black man. The Ku Klux Klan then burnt down the village of Rosewood, Florida, in which almost all of the people were black. The robbery was never proved.

A Cartoon from *Judge* magazine, 16 August 1924, published under the caption 'It seems there was a negro and an Irishman and a Jew ...'

B A black victim of the Ku Klux Klan remembers their activities.

After us coloured folks was considered free and turned loose the Ku Klux Klan broke out. Some coloured people started farming and gathered old stock. If they got so they made good money and had a good farm, the Ku Klux would come and murder them ... There was a coloured man called Jim Freeman. They destroyed his stuff and him because he was making some money. They hung him on a tree in his front yard, right in front of his cabin.

C A member of the Ku Klux Klan in the 1920s explains why he joined and what he hoped the Klan would do.

It is going to drive the bootleggers forever out of the land. It is going to bring clean moving pictures, clean literature ... break up roadside parking ... enforce the floggings.

D Members of the Ku Klux Klan. Note the white robes and hoods.

When the Governor of Indiana refused to pardon him, Stevenson produced evidence of illegal Klan activities which sent a Congressman and other officials to prison.

The Klan had drawn support from poor whites. Its appeal weakened when the economy began to recover in the early 1920s. Support for the Klan did not die out completely. It still has supporters in some parts of the USA, even today.

E A historian looks at the reasons for the growth of the Klan (from *America: A Narrative History* by G B Tindall, 1992).

The new Klan was determined to protect its warped notion of the American way of life, not only from African Americans, but also from Roman Catholics, Jews and other immigrants.

The Klan was no longer restricted to the South. It flourished mainly among the uprooted and insecure newcomers to the cities and towns. The robes, the flaming crosses, the strange processions, the kneeling recruits – all tapped a deep American urge towards mystery and brought drama into the dreary routine of a thousand communities. At the same time the Klan was a reaction against the strange and exotic, against shifting moral standards, the declining influence of churches, the broadmindedness of cities and colleges. In the south west, it became more than anything else a moral crusade.

Q

1 What can you tell about the Ku Klux Klan from source D?
2 Who supported the Ku Klux Klan and why? Using the information on page 14, copy the chart and complete it with as many examples as you can think of. The first one has been done for you.

People	Reasons for supporting the Ku Klux Klan
People who hated Jews	The Klan claimed that the Jews were enemies of the USA. The Klan beat up Jews.

3 What do you think the author of source E meant by writing that the Klan was determined 'to protect its warped notion of the American way of life'?
4 Why do you think so little was done to stop the Ku Klux Klan?
5 Look back at pages 10 to 15 and explain how far you agree with this interpretation: 'Support for the Ku Klux Klan proves that America was a very racist society in the 1920s.'

Prohibition

Why was prohibition introduced and what were its effects? Why did gangsters and crime flourish during this time? The prohibition laws were finally repealed in 1933. Why did Americans change their minds about prohibition?

What was prohibition?

In January 1919 the 18th Amendment to the United States Constitution was passed. This Amendment banned the sale and transport of alcohol. The Volstead Act of January 1920 backed this up by explaining that 'liquor' was any drink which contained 0.5 per cent alcohol. Most beers, for example, usually contained at least five per cent alcohol. The USA went 'dry' when the new law came into effect on 16 January 1920.

Who led the fight for prohibition?

Opposition to alcohol was not a new idea. Many immigrants had strong religious feelings which led them to disapprove of alcohol. Groups such as the Women's Christian Temperance Union and the Anti-Saloon League had campaigned against alcohol for many years.

By 1910 the Anti-Saloon League was a well organised group, particularly in the countryside. It got the support of Protestant churches to encourage people to vote for 'dry' candidates. This was so successful that by 1916 there were a large number of 'dry' supporters in Congress. In 1917 the USA entered the First World War.

Why was the First World War important for prohibition?

Wars sometimes bring about changes in society. The First World War helped bring about the prohibition of alcohol in America.

During the war there were new calls for prohibition to help the war effort. Brewing used up the equivalent of 11 million loaves of barley a day. This could have been used to feed the USA's **Allies**. The Food and Fuel Control Act was brought in to ban the use of grain for brewing alcohol.

Some people thought that because the brewing firms Pabst and Busch were German (the USA's enemy in the war), they should be avoided. It was also claimed that alcohol stopped American soldiers from firing straight, so it was seen as a patriotic duty to support prohibition.

A Poster showing a boy being led by his Guardian Angel along the right path.

During the war local prohibition laws were passed in states all over the USA. By 1918 nearly 75 per cent of Americans were living in parts of the USA which were already 'dry'.

Opponents of prohibition

There were of course different points of view about how harmful alcohol was. Some people thought that alcohol was useful as a medicine, others simply enjoyed getting drunk! The problem was that the supporters of prohibition seemed to be better organised than their opponents. Organised resistance to the 'drys' only began in 1918 when W H Stayton founded the Association Against the Prohibition Amendment (AAPA). He got financial support from the brewers and distillers, but they had begun organising too late to stop prohibition.

Daddy's in There---

And Our Shoes and Stockings and Clothes and Food Are in There, Too, and They'll Never Come out.

B This poster, showing two children standing outside a saloon, was issued by the Anti-Saloon League. It first appeared in the Chicago *Sun Times* during prohibition.

C A supporter of prohibition describes the evils of alcohol in a speech given in Congress.

Scientific research has demonstrated that alcohol is a poison, it lowers to an appalling degree the character of our citizens, thereby weakening public morals and democracy, [it] produces widespread crime, poverty and insanity, inflicts disease and untimely death upon hundreds and thousands of citizens, and leads to their children being born handicapped.

D Was prohibition an attack by small town America on the evils of the big city? This is a quotation from *The Anti-Saloon Yearbook*, 1914 by Purley A Baker.

The evils of the cities have been the undoing of past empires and civilizations. Already some of our cities are endangered by an unpatriotic element which is manipulated by un-American drink and by the kind of politician the saloon creates. The saloon stands for the worst in political life. All who stand for the best must stand against it. If America is to be saved the liquor traffic must be destroyed.

E A historian describes an argument for prohibition put forward by Southern racists (from *Prohibition – The Era of Excess* by Andrew Sinclair, 1962).

Prohibition was a way of keeping the Negro in his place. Since the vote and alcohol were the two ways in which the Negro could stand up for himself, they were denied to him. By 1917 all the Southern states had discriminated against the Negro voter and all except two had passed prohibition laws against alcohol. Prohibition gained a foothold in the South and was made possible only after the voting rights of the Negro had been restricted.

1 Look at source A. Make a list of the 'dangers' that the boy is being led away from.
2 How would each of the posters in sources A and B have encouraged Americans to support the prohibition of alcohol?
3 Which of the posters do you think would have had the greatest impact on the American public at that time? Give reasons for your answer.
4 'Source B is of no value to a historian because it is so biased.' Do you agree? Explain your answer.
5 a) Why was prohibition introduced? Copy the chart and complete as much of it as you can.

Cause	Explanation
Patriotic reasons	
Religious reasons	
Effects on families	
Effects on health	

b) Were any of the causes linked? Why, for example, might religious reasons and effects on families be linked together?

BOOTLEGGING

Problems in enforcing prohibition

John Kramer was the first Prohibition Commissioner. His job was to make sure that the prohibition law was obeyed. He boasted that the prohibition law would be obeyed in cities large and small, and where it was not obeyed it would be enforced. He promised that alcohol would not be made or sold.

Congress gave Kramer $2.2 million to help him enforce the law. This paid for 1500 prohibition agents. It soon became clear that this would not be enough. Speakeasies began to appear in many parts of the country. By 1926 the amount spent enforcing prohibition had risen to $10 million. By 1928 there were thought to be at least 30 000 speakeasies in New York alone. In 1929 the new Prohibition Commissioner James Doran told Congress that a serious attempt to enforce prohibition would cost $300 million. He was given $12 million.

There were problems about deciding which alcohol was legal and which wasn't. Alcohol could still be produced for certain medicines and 'industrial alcohol' was used by a number of firms. The government ordered companies to put substances in the industrial alcohol to stop it being drunk, but clever criminals got round these rules and large quantities of industrial alcohol found their way into the speakeasies.

It was difficult to stop the smuggling of alcohol. The USA has 30 000 kilometres of coastline and land borders. Neither Canada, which borders the USA to the north, nor Mexico, to the south, were 'dry' countries. There were many places where drink could be brought in without detection.

Judge Alfred J Talley was angry that relatively few people were sent to prison in New York for breaking the prohibition law. Between 1921 and 1924, for example, a total of 6904 cases of breaking the prohibition law were brought before New York's Grand Jury. As many as 6074 of these cases were dismissed and there were only 20

Bootlegging got its name in the 17th century, when the British ruled parts of North America. The British made people pay a tax on drink. Smugglers used to hide drink in their high leather boots, so as to avoid the taxes.

convictions. Judge Talley said that as a result of prohibition the United States had become 'the most lawless country on the face of the earth'. When he asked the Grand Jurors to explain why there were so few convictions, the foreman said: 'The men tell me that they will not convict men for offences which they themselves are committing.' It is difficult to enforce a law which large numbers of people are prepared to break. Right from the start there were very large numbers of people – particularly in the cities – who were prepared to defy the prohibition law. American citizens got used to seeing people driving lorries laden with beer barrels in broad daylight through busy cities – with the police and prohibition agents apparently doing nothing to stop them.

A A historian examines the causes of crime in the USA in the 1920s (quoted from *A History of the United States* by C P Hill, 1974).

Drinking, largely because it was forbidden, became fashionable. Prohibition was the chief cause of a great increase in crimes of every kind, and especially in crimes of violence. In bootlegging, as in every great industry, rivalry grew and disputes became more bitter, just because the profits at stake were so great. Other big industries could settle their disputes in court; bootlegging, being illegal, could not … Bootlegging, being an illegal business, inevitably attracted criminals. Prohibition was not the only cause of the outbreak of crime which followed. Modern inventions, especially the automobile and the machine gun, were admirably suited to the gangster's work. All these factors encouraged crime. But prohibition and the resultant growth of bootlegging were undoubtedly its chief causes.

Year	Drunks	Disorderly conduct	Drivers	Alcoholics	Total
1920	14 313	6 097	–	33	20 443
1921	21 850	5 232	494	33	27 609
1922	36 299	7 925	472	50	44 746
1923	45 226	8 076	645	177	54 124
1924	47 805	6 404	683	874	55 766
1925	51 361	5 522	820	814	58 517

B Arrests for drinking offences in Philadelphia, 1920–25. (These figures are from the Philadelphia Police Department.)

C A painting by Ben Shahn (1934) showing a number of devices used by bootleggers to avoid detection.

CHARRED KE

D The American writer, Frederick Lewis Allen, explains why the prohibition agents were not successful (from *Only Yesterday: An Informal History of the 1920s*, 1931):

Anybody who believed that men employable at thirty-five or forty or fifty dollars a week would surely have the expert technical knowledge and diligence to supervise successfully the complicated chemical operations of industrial-alcohol plants or to outwit the craftiest devices of smugglers and bootleggers, and that they would surely have the force of character to resist corruption by men whose pockets were bulging with money, would be ready to believe also in Santa Claus, perpetual motion and pixies.

Q

1 Look at source C. Make a list of the ways in which the bootleggers are hiding the drink.
2 Look at source A. Why was prohibition likely to lead to more violent crimes?
3 What problems did the prohibition agents face when they tried to stop people making and drinking alcohol? Make a list.
4 Read source B.
   a) If you wanted to show that prohibition led to an increase in crime, which figures from source B would you use?
   b) What are the problems in relying on source B to prove that prohibition led to an increase in crime? (Think about where these statistics come from.)

GANGSTERS

Organised crime did not begin with prohibition. Organised gambling and prostitution had been connected to saloons for many years. Prohibition, however, gave criminals a chance to make vast fortunes from the illegal alcohol trade.

Until about 1923 businessmen hired small gangs to protect their breweries. After 1923 bigger and more ruthless gangs developed in the cities. They controlled the production and supply of alcohol. They made use of new forms of communication – such as the telephone – to organise crime across the country.

Al Capone

The most famous of the gangsters was Al Capone, whose gang eventually gained control of organised crime in Chicago. At the height of his success in the late 1920s he is thought to have made between $60 million and $100 million a year from the beer trade. He is also thought to have owned banks, restaurants and other businesses. His nickname was 'Scarface'. He wore the smartest suits and rode around in a huge bulletproof car.

He employed about 1000 men in a sort of private army which controlled his 'businesses' in alcohol, prostitution and protection rackets. A racket was a type of blackmail. Gangsters threatened to smash up the shops or businesses of people who refused to pay them 'protection money'. The most famous example of the power of Capone's private army was the Saint Valentine's Day Massacre of 1929, when the rival Bugs Moran gang was wiped out in a hail of machine-gun fire. Moran had killed one of Capone's friends. On 14 February seven members of the Moran gang were killed at their meeting place in North Clark Street, Chicago. Moran only escaped because he arrived at the meeting place a few minutes late. Nobody was ever convicted of the crime.

A 'Prohibition Alley', circa 1934, a painting by Ben Shahn. Look for: (1) The iron gates of the speakeasy; (2) Rich people waiting to go into the speakeasy; (3) A diagram showing how to make illegal alcohol; (4) A ship which has brought in the illegal alcohol; (5) Barrels of whiskey, smuggled in by ship; (6) A painting on an alley wall, showing the gangster Al Capone; (7) A victim of gang warfare, lying on the pavement.

The government seemed to be helpless to stop gangsters such as Capone from breaking the law and getting away with it. This weakened respect for the prohibition law. It was common knowledge that many of the people who were supposed to be stopping the gangsters were actually taking bribes from them.

Capone is thought to have beaten to death a number of people and ordered the execution of many men who stood in his way, but the authorities could not get enough evidence against him – and witnesses to his crimes were not prepared to speak up in court. Eventually a Treasury agent infiltrated his gang and Capone was finally imprisoned in 1931 – for not paying his taxes.

B 'The National Gesture', a cartoon drawn by Clive Weed. It appeared in *Judge* magazine on 12 June 1926.

C Charlie Berns, interviewed just before his death in 1971, remembers running a speakeasy in the 1920s in New York:

Every speakeasy had to make some arrangements with the cops to survive. In our case it wasn't exactly a showdown, nothing on a regular basis, more like an act of friendship. We would slip the captain a $50 bill from time to time and a box of cigars to the cops on the beat. They could always count on us for free meals and drinks, and at Christmas time, of course, we had a gift for everybody.

Speakeasies got their name from the fact that drinkers had to keep their voices down or 'speak easily' to the door keeper on guard in order to get in without being observed.

D A policeman in Chicago in the 1920s remembers the problems of carrying out the prohibition laws:

I was first sent to a Polish neighbourhood and the saloon keepers would always welcome you. You couldn't pay for anything. The bottle was there and you were supposed to drink.

We were just ordinary policemen and if you did anything in the way of enforcement they'd put you on a job where there was nothing but weeds. It was a conspiracy and the higher ups were being taken care of.

I was assigned to 12th Street and Halstead. I was going up and down and I backed into a doorway to see what was going on. A fella dashed up to me and said, 'This is for you.' He handed me an envelope, I took it and he was gone. I opened it up and there was $75 in it.

The payoff was such a common thing. Believe me, I never went out seeking it. It just came as a matter of course. I tried to do my job. We went out on several raids and made convictions, but the whole thing was so common. It was laughable.

1 Make a list of important events in the life of Al Capone.
2 What is happening in source A? What does the artist think about prohibition?
3 Look at source B.
  a) What do you think the cartoonist meant by 'the national gesture'?
  b) Choose three of the groups of people identified and explain why it was so useful for the gangsters to have them on their side.
4 Compare the interpretations in sources C and D of how the police got on with the people who ran the speakeasies:
  a) What similarities do you notice?
  b) What differences do you notice?
  c) What reasons can you suggest for the different interpretations?
5 Using all the information and sources, suggest reasons why gangsters such as Al Capone were so successful.

WHY WAS PROHIBITION ENDED?

The campaign against prohibition

The brewers and distillers fought prohibition because it cost them money and put many of them out of business. They were, of course, not the only opponents of prohibition. Immigrants, from countries such as Ireland and Germany, found that when they arrived in the USA, they were no longer allowed to drink. They resented this change to their way of life.

Hotel owners who were angry about losing business joined the Association Against the Prohibition Amendment (AAPA). Other groups were set up to fight prohibition. The Moderation League, for example, wanted the law to be changed because it was not clear enough and therefore did not work properly. It wanted 'a reasonable and working definition of intoxicating liquors'. The Voluntary Committee of Lawyers claimed that prohibition was against the American Constitution because it threatened the American people's freedoms.

Groups representing soldiers and workers also opposed prohibition. The American Legion

A The President of the American Federation of Labor, Samuel Gompers, made a statement to the Senate Judiciary Committee Inquiry into Prohibition in 1929 warning about the dangers of denying American workers the right to have a drink.

Depriving the American workingman of his glass of beer tends to promote industrial unrest and discontent [unhappiness]. Already in Detroit the radicals were gaining support in the factories. These unfair laws breed communism.

B A historian of prohibition discusses the reasons why rich businessmen opposed prohibition (from *Ardent Spirits: The Rise and Fall of Prohibition* by John Kobler, 1973).

The defence of the Constitution was not the only motive. Between 1916 and 1921 the taxes collected by the federal government had increased sixfold. It occurred to the Du Ponts that to restore legal alcohol (and its accompanying tax) would eliminate the tax burden. This alcohol tax would be enough to pay off the entire debt of the United States in a little less than fifteen years. Irenee Du Pont believed that a tax on beer would save just one of the family companies $10 000 000.

objected to it because prohibition was leading people to lose respect for the law. The American Federation of Labor felt that people were entitled to a drink after a day's work. Their slogan was: 'No beer, no work'.

Rich industrialists also joined the campaign against prohibition. The Du Pont brothers had made a fortune in the armaments industry. At first they had been supporters of prohibition, but they said that they joined the AAPA because they were worried about prohibition's threat to personal freedom. Another possible reason why rich businessmen might want to get rid of prohibition can be found in source B.

The Prince of Wales visited the USA in 1925. He was well aware of how easy it was to get alcohol. When asked what he thought of prohibition he replied, 'Great! When does it begin!'

Women

Some were surprised to find that women got involved in the campaign against prohibition. Women had played an important part in the Anti-Saloon League and had been granted the vote in the year following the introduction of prohibition. Many people thought, therefore, that now women had the vote they would use it to block any attempts to end prohibition. Clarence Darrow, an opponent of prohibition, said that you might as well wait until Halley's Comet returns – or talk about taking your summer holidays on Mars – rather than think about repealing prohibition.

However, in 1929 Pauline Sabin founded the Women's Organization for National Prohibition Reform. She was intelligent, attractive and rich. She was a member of the 'Manhattan smart set' – the most fashionable members of New York high society. These people went to parties where alcohol was a topic of conversation. Drinking was fashionable amongst the richer classes. It seemed absurd to ban something so popular.

Pauline Sabin made witty speeches in which she attacked prohibition – and the dull, boring ladies who supported the Anti-Saloon League. When she said she was going to fight prohibition the letters poured in from women all over the country. She realised that there was a large group of women waiting to be organised. By 1932 there were a million members.

The tactics of the AAPA

The AAPA used similar methods in its campaign to get rid of prohibition to those used by the Anti-Saloon League when it tried to introduce prohibition.

- It backed 'wet' candidates (opponents to prohibition) for political jobs.
- It advertised its ideas in newspapers and magazines.
- It criticised the opposition – in this case the leaders of the Anti-Saloon League.
- It produced its own books, cartoons and pamphlets. These blamed prohibition for almost every social problem – from disease to poverty, unemployment and crime.

The Depression and the campaign against prohibition

Many ordinary voters became opponents of prohibition because it turned many decent people who simply wanted an occasional drink into law breakers. This was particularly noticeable in the Depression, when so many people had lost their jobs. It seemed to be a better idea to legalise alcohol and collect badly needed taxes from alcohol than to let gangsters make millions from breaking a law which no longer worked.

In 1929 President Hoover set up the Wickersham Commission to look at the working of the prohibition law. Its report, issued in 1931, confirmed what almost everybody knew – that the prohibition law did not work. In the 1932 election campaign the **Democrat** candidate, FD Roosevelt, opposed prohibition. He won the election and in 1933 the prohibition law was repealed (abolished).

D 'The King Still Reigns', a cartoon published in the *Baltimore Sun*, 1930.

C An anti-prohibition demonstration.

After prohibition

- The number of speakeasies in New York fell from about 32 000 in 1929 to about 9000 in 1933.
- Bootlegging was unnecessary – but crime didn't stop. Criminals switched their attentions to other ways of making money.
- Gangsters were no longer needed to help the public get a drink. Public opinion turned against the gangsters. Capone was not the only crime boss sent to jail.

1 Who was against prohibition and why? Copy the chart and complete it with as many examples as you can find. The first one has been done for you.

Group	Reason for opposition to prohibition
Brewers and distillers	It cost them money and put many of them out of business
Rich businessmen	
Working men	
American Legion	
Supporters of personal freedom	
Women opponents of prohibition	

2 How did the following help cause the end of prohibition:
   a) the tactics of the AAPA; b) the Depression;
   c) women; d) gangsters; e) problems in enforcing prohibition; f) other reasons?
3 What do you think the person who drew source D was trying to 'say' about gangsters? Back up your answer by describing the cartoon carefully.
4 Now look back through this unit (pages 16–23) and explain whether you agree with this interpretation: 'Prohibition was doomed from the start.' Give reasons for your answer.

The USA – An Economic Giant?

Why was the American economy so strong during the 1920s and how useful are statistics in measuring this? Advertising was very important to the economy. Why was this and what methods were used? The use of mass production made people like Henry Ford very rich. What effect did his methods have on the American economy?

Politicians are often seen on our television screens, arguing about the state of the economy. Sometimes they back up their claims by quoting sets of figures. But how do we know what's really happening? How do we 'measure' the country's economic strength? The figures in this unit give clues about the American economy in the 1920s.

The First World War

The American economy was in a powerful position at the end of the First World War, compared with its European rivals. Much of the fighting had been in Europe – and none of it in the USA. France, Britain, Germany and Russia had been exhausted by the war. Many countries ended up borrowing large sums of money from the USA. American bankers and businessmen were in a good position to invest money in Europe – and make money when the European economies recovered. Some of the American money was pumped into western European factories. When the factories made profits the American investors did well.

Buying shares

Many Americans dreamed of becoming rich by making a big profit on the Wall Street Stock Exchange. This would be done by buying shares in a company. If the company made money you would get a share in the profits. These shares (or stocks) would then be worth more, so you could sell them at a higher price on the Stock Exchange. Many people borrowed money to buy shares in the hope that share prices would carry on going up.

Government policy

The **Republican** governments of the 1920s tried to help businessmen by protecting trade. This was done by putting a tariff (tax) on goods brought into the USA from abroad. This meant that foreign goods cost more money, and American businessmen might not have to face so much competition from foreign traders. This policy was called protectionism.

Calvin Coolidge

He was President of the USA from 1923 to 1929. Coolidge believed that: 'The business of America is business.' Coolidge's Republican Party gave as much help to businessmen as it could. The taxes which businessmen had to pay were lowered and businessmen were encouraged to get on with the job of making money with as little interference from the government as possible. Coolidge summed up his ideas about business when he said:

	1880 (%)	1900 (%)	1913 (%)	1928 (%)
Britain	23	19	14	10
United States	15	24	32	39
Germany	9	13	15	12
France	8	7	6	6
Russia	8	9	8	5
Austria-Hungary	4	5	4	–
Italy	3	3	2	3
Rest of world	30	20	19	25

A This table shows the major countries' share of output of manufactured goods (goods made by machines) in the period 1880 to 1928. The bigger the percentage the more industrialised the country.

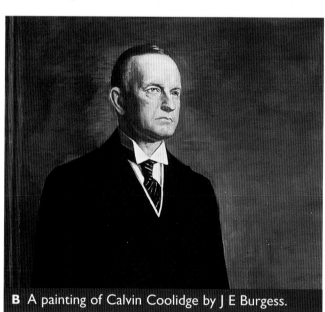

B A painting of Calvin Coolidge by J E Burgess.

'The man who builds a factory builds a temple. The man who works there worships there.'

Workers were not encouraged to join trade unions. The government often sided with the bosses when there were strikes.

> Calvin Coolidge's nickname was 'Silent Cal' because he didn't say much. A White House guest told Coolidge that she had bet that she could make him say three words. He replied: 'You lose.'

	National Income	Population	Per Capita Income
United States	$37 billion	98 million	$377
Britain	11	45	244
France	6	39	153
Japan	2	55	36
Germany	12	65	184
Italy	4	37	108
Russia	7	171	41
Austria-Hungary	3	52	57

C This table shows the national income (see source C on page 33), population and per capita income of the Powers in 1914. (Per capita income is the amount of wealth produced in a country divided by the number of people in it. Therefore Russia was actually a poorer country than Italy, even though it had a higher national income in 1914.)

	1890	1900	1910	1913	1920	1930	1938
United States	147	248	483	541	694	762	697
Britain	145	171	185	195	212	184	196
Germany	71	112	158	187	159	177	228
France	36	48	55	63	65	98	84
Austria-Hungary	20	29	40	49	–	–	–
Russia	11	30	41	54	14	65	177
Japan	5	5	15	23	34	56	97
Italy	5	5	10	11	14	24	28

D This table shows the energy consumption of the Powers, 1890–1938. Industrialised countries use up more energy than less industrialised countries. The energy measured here is in millions of tonnes of coal used.

E An American historian gives reasons for the success of the American economy (from *America in the Twentieth Century*, edited by J T Patterson, 3rd edition, 1989).

The years between 1917 and 1929 saw industrial breakthroughs. New machines revolutionised the construction industry, including power shovels, concrete mixers and dump trucks. The communications industries developed automatic switchboards and dial phones. Consumer goods industries boomed as never before. Moderately priced products included radios, wristwatches, cigarette lighters, hand cameras, vacuum cleaners and washing machines.

F A British historian looks at the USA's economy (from *The Rise and Fall of the Great Powers* by Paul Kennedy, 1988).

The USA seemed to have all the economic advantages which some of the other powers possessed in part, but none of their disadvantages. It was huge, but the vast distances were shortened by some 400 000 kilometres of railway in 1914 (compared with Russia's 74 000 kilometres spread over an area two and a half times as large). The sheer size of the area under cultivation, the efficiency of its farm machinery, the decreasing costs of transport (because of railways and steamships) made American wheat, corn, pork, beef and other products cheaper than any in Europe. American firms were equal to or better than any in the world; and they enjoyed an enormous domestic market, which their European rivals did not.

In industry and agriculture and communications there was both efficiency and size.

1 What can you tell from each of the sets of figures (sources A, C and D) about:
   a) the American economy in the 1920s compared with other countries;
   b) how the American economy was changing;
   c) whether the American economy was changing more quickly or slowly than other countries?
   Remember to back up each answer with figures.

2 What can you work out about the American economy from the written sources (E and F) that you can't from the figures (A, C and D)? Give as many examples as you can.

3 'In the late 1920s the United States was the world's greatest economic power but the other powers were catching up.' Using sources A to F explain whether you agree or disagree with this interpretation.

ADVERTISING

A An advertisement placed in *Life* magazine by advertisers who wanted to show the benefits of advertising.

In the 19th century many firms sold their goods to people in the local area and therefore did not think they needed to advertise country-wide. This changed in the early 20th century, when mass production allowed firms to produce huge numbers of goods and sell them across the country. Firms such as Coca-Cola showed that they could make huge profits by spending money on advertising

Even the President was convinced of the value of advertising. Calvin Coolidge said that: 'Advertising makes new thoughts, new desires, new actions. It is the most powerful influence in adapting and changing the habits and way of life, affecting what we eat, what we wear and the work and play of a whole nation.'

campaigns. The more they spent on advertisements, the bigger the profit they seemed to make.

In 1918 American firms spent about $58.5 million on advertising in magazines. This figure rose to $129.5 million in 1920 and to nearly $200 million by 1929. Advertising played a very important part in keeping the American economy growing in the 1920s.

Methods of advertising

Firms began to take advertising very seriously because they realised that it could help them make big profits. The people who designed the advertisements studied psychology to find out what methods were most likely to persuade people to buy things. J B Watson was a Professor of Psychology who gave up his college job to be an advertising boss. He believed that people were easy to influence if you chose your advertisements carefully. J Walter Thompson was another successful advertising boss. He once said that the average American consumer had the mind of a '14-year-old human animal'.

Different approaches were used in different advertisements. Some advertisements were designed to make people worry – for example, about spots, dandruff, oily skin or wrinkles. The advertiser's products could then be sold as a way of helping people get over their worries. In 1921 the Lambert Company used a word which sounded rather serious, *halitosis*, for bad breath in an advertisement for Listerine mouthwash. The advertisement was so successful that sales rose within six years from 100 000 bottles to four million a year.

B An advertising boss explains how advertisements should appeal to women (quoted in *Growing Up with Advertising* by J H Appel, 1940).

Nine tenths of the goods bought annually are bought by women. Woman is a creature of the imagination. We pay her a compliment when we say this, for imagination comes from the feelings and feelings come from the heart.

And so the advertising appeal, to reach women, must not ignore the first great quality of the heart, which is love. Most advertisers do not ignore the quality of love. There, in almost every advertisement, is a reference, in word or picture, to mother love, to the home, to children, to sentiment.

While it might be unwise to mix too much sentiment and imagination with reason in an advertisement to reach men, there can hardly be too much imagination in an advertisement to reach women. Even vanity comes from the heart and vanity buys many goods.

Perfume companies looked at the methods used by other firms and realised that they could make even bigger profits by advertising. The perfume advertisements portrayed an exciting and glamorous world, often showing attractive and elegant women dressed in expensive clothes (see source C below). These advertisements appeared in magazines and newspapers. Some of the women who bought the new magazines (see source B on page 6) were from families that had done quite well in the 1920s and had money to spend.

Once people had bought all they could be persuaded to buy, or could afford to buy, what would then happen to the American economy?

D This advertisement for Franklin cars appeared in the *Saturday Evening Post* on June 22, 1929. It is interesting that the advertisement is appealing to women drivers.

C A perfume advertisement from 1920.

HENRY FORD AND MASS PRODUCTION

Henry Ford was an electrical engineer who dreamed of producing cars which were cheap enough for ordinary people to buy. At first banks refused to lend him money because they thought his dreams were not realistic. He built his first car in a rented brick shed.

In 1909 he introduction his Model T Ford, the 'tin lizzie' in 'any colour as long as it's black'. By concentrating on building one simple car he managed to bring its price down from $950 to $550.

The magic belt

The real breakthrough came with the idea of mass production and the use of the 'magic belt'. Before the days of mass production most cars were made up in small workshops. The workers wasted a lot of time walking about, getting tools and bringing pieces of equipment to the car. In 1914 Henry Ford opened his new factory at Highland Park, Michigan. It was the first car factory to include the 'magic belt'.

Henry Ford copied the assembly line methods used in meat packing factories and slaughter houses (see source A). An electric conveyor belt carried the partly assembled car at the same speed past workers who stood at the same spot and did just one job. The tools and equipment the worker needed to do his job were brought to him so he didn't need to waste as much time. Small parts were slid on wires from one work bench to another.

In 1913 it had taken Ford workers about 14 hours to assemble a Model T. With the magic belt they could do it in 93 minutes. In 1914 Ford produced 45 per cent of all cars made in the USA. By 1925 Ford produced a complete car every 10 seconds. The system gave Americans a simple car at

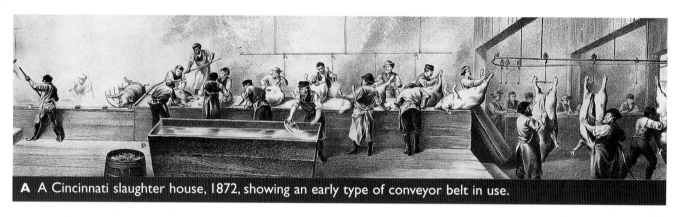

A A Cincinnati slaughter house, 1872, showing an early type of conveyor belt in use.

B Production line at a Ford factory, about 1914, showing workers assembling flywheels.

an affordable price. It was in Ford's interest at first to make just one type of car because it allowed him to keep the production line going with massive supplies of materials and parts.

Other car manufacturers copied Ford's methods. Soon many different types of car were being built on such belts. Huge numbers of jobs were created in the new car factories and the industries which supplied them – Detroit, for example, was known as 'Motortown' and gave its name to the Detroit based record label Tamla Motown.

The car industry created a huge demand for oil – and therefore helped the oil industry to grow quickly. In the 1920s the motor vehicle was consuming annually 90 per cent of the country's petroleum products, 80 per cent of the rubber, 29 per cent of the steel, 75 per cent of the plate glass and 24 per cent of the machine tools. The demand for cars was stimulated by advertising.

Ford made cars which were cheap enough for the ordinary person in the street to afford. The figures in source C show you the huge increase in the number of cars and in the amount of roads. Think about the effect of these changes.

	1920	1929
Kilometres of surfaced roads	620 000	1 000 000
Motor cars on the roads	9 000 000	26 000 000

C The rise of the car, showing a dramatic increase in just ten years.

D The rise of the car changed a whole way of life, as these comments from Alistair Cooke's *America* show (1973):

Ford believed in supplying conveniences for the many, rather than service for the few. It was a belief which led straight to paper towels and cafeterias and super-markets and motels.

It is staggering to consider what the Model T was to lead to. It certainly wove the first network of paved highways. Most of all, the Model T gave to the farmer and rancher, miles from anywhere, a new pair of legs.

The automobile has ended the old distinction between town and country. Nowhere is this more obvious than in Los Angeles. It was the first city built for the automobile and its needs – by freeways, highways, garages, gas stations, car lots, parking lots. And all of it is blanketed with foul air.

E Mass production methods had far-reaching effects (from *History of the American Economy* by G M Walton and R M Robertson, 1994).

The Ford plant adopted the 'moving assembly' that had long been used in the manufacture of simple products. Before 1920 the moving assembly had spread throughout the automobile industry, the electrical industry and the budding household appliance industry, as well as to food processing and cigarette manufacture.

All of this brought a change in the idea of management. It became more and more obvious that good managers would be men trained in the sciences, in schools of engineering and in the new school of business administration.

As automobiles came into common use after 1910, large towns and cities gained business at the expense of small towns and villages; by 1920 shops in cities were beginning to attract customers from distances not even imagined 10 years earlier. This change was seen in new ways of distributing and marketing goods.

F 'Get off the earth', the front cover of the American magazine *Life* in 1923.

Get off the earth!

Q

1 Describe what is happening in sources A and B. How is the way of working similar?
2 In what ways was the 'magic belt' an improvement on previous methods of making cars?
3 The following industries all grew in the 1920s because of the rapid increase in car production. Copy the chart and then fill in the column on the right to explain the connection between them. One has been done for you.

Industries	Connection to the automobile industry
Oil	
Rubber	
Steel	
Glass	
Construction	Roads, petrol stations, roadside diners were just a few of the things which had to be built for the new car industry.

4 Work in pairs. One of you should write an obituary (an article about someone after they have died) for Henry Ford from the point of view of someone who thinks that mass production of cars has been a good thing. The other should write an obituary for Ford from the point of view of someone who thinks that the mass production of cars has been a bad thing. Then together write an explanation of why your obituaries are so different.

The Wall Street Crash and the Depression

Why did the Wall Street Stock Exchange crash and what effect did the Depression have on Americans? Were all Americans equally hit by the Depression?

Speculators

We saw on page 24 that many Americans speculated (gambled) that if they borrowed money to buy shares on New York's Wall Street Stock Exchange they could make a quick profit by selling the shares when their value went up. It seemed an easy way to make money. Millions of people – from bankers to shoeshine boys – seemed to be playing the Stock Market. The value of shares rose because people kept buying shares. The problem was that the value of shares could go down as well as up. It all depended on how well the company you invested in was doing. Once your company stopped making good profits its shares tended to go down. All was well as long as the economy was booming and wages were high.

Herbert Hoover

Herbert Hoover was President of the USA from 1929 to 1933. He was elected by a huge majority and promised to put 'a chicken in every pot and a car in every garage'. Hoover was a Republican and followed Coolidge's policy of keeping government out of business.

Hoover's first job had been an office boy, but he eventually became a millionaire. He believed that government should encourage business so that other Americans could follow his example and earn themselves fortunes. He had great confidence that Americans would continue to enjoy the highest standard of living in the world.

Inequality

If you look at the sections on women and black people (pages 8 and 10) you will see that millions of Americans did not share in the boom years of the 1920s. Farm workers, for example, found that prices of crops fell because other countries produced those crops more cheaply. Millions of unskilled labourers could not afford to buy the new cars, radios and fridges. These people faced a desperate struggle for survival. In 1929 nearly half of all American families were on low incomes (earning less than $1500 a year).

Trouble on Wall Street

In the summer of 1929 a number of richer shareholders began to sell their shares. Maybe they were not confident that the value of shares could keep rising. Prices began to fall in September. On 19 October a number of nervous dealers sold large blocks of shares. Two days later prices fell sharply. On 24 October there was a panic to sell shares before they became worthless. More than 12 million shares were sold on the 'day the dam burst'. Very few people wanted to buy.

There was another huge panic on 'Black Tuesday', 29 October, when more than 16 million shares were sold on Wall Street. This became known as the Wall Street Crash – the day the Stock Market collapsed. People who had borrowed money to buy shares watched helplessly as the prices of their shares fell. Some people were ruined overnight. In only one day, for example, the shares of Union Cigar fell from $113 each to just $4 each.

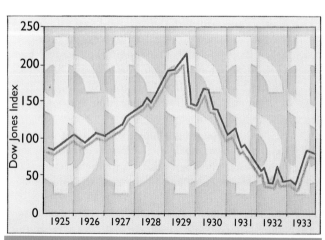

A The Dow Jones index is used to show the average price of shares on the Wall Street Stock Exchange. This graph shows the rise and fall in share prices, 1925–33. Notice the steep drop in 1929 at the time of the Wall Street Crash.

Suicide

For some people the shock of the Wall Street Crash was just too much for them to bear. The president of Union Cigar committed suicide by jumping from a hotel window ledge. An old couple who had lost everything killed themselves because it was too late for them to start life again.

Poverty

The businessman Arthur Robertson remembered that people who before the crash had driven around in expensive cars now walked around Wall Street like zombies, unable even to pay a bus fare. Others tried to raise some money by selling their homes – but nobody wanted to buy.

In November 1929 the panic ended when very rich men, such as the oil billionaire J D Rockefeller, bought shares. If you look at source A, however, you can see that share prices continued to fall for a long time.

B The problem of overproduction.

The Problem of Overproduction

In 1927 a few people saw that there might be problems ahead.

Fewer products such as cars were being sold.

SALES

Sales fell and bosses cut prices and wages.

NOW ONLY $600

When this didn't work they cut costs by sacking workers.

ADDED £100 TAX ON CARS   EXPORT

This was partly caused by overproduction. Factories had produced more goods than Americans could afford to buy.

They couldn't sell many goods abroad because foreign countries put taxes on American goods.

This meant there were fewer workers with less money to buy goods, so factories cut costs again and more people lost their jobs.

C A historian looks at some of the weaknesses of the American economy in the 1920s (from *America: Past and Present*, 4th edition, by Divine, Breen, Fredrickson and Williams, 1995).

The economic system failed to share out wealth fairly. Too much money went into profits and industrial expansion, and not enough went into the hands of the workers, who were also the consumers. Factory production increased 43 per cent during the 1920s, but the wages of industrial workers only rose 11 per cent. If the billions that went into stock market speculation had been used instead to increase wages, this would have given consumers more spending power.

Q

1 Make a timeline of events mentioned in this unit.
2 Look at source A.
   a) In which year did share prices reach their highest point?
   b) 'Share prices increased gradually during the 1920s.' Do you agree? Give figures from the graph shown in Source A in your answer.
3 Look at source B. What does it suggest about how each of the following harmed the American economy: (a) overproduction; (b) foreign taxes; (c) wage cuts.
4 a) Which one of the reasons listed in question 3 (overproduction, foreign taxes, wage cuts) can also be found in source C?
   b) Which one of these reasons do you think had the most harmful effects on the economy? Explain your answer.

THE DEPRESSION

Unemployment

In the months which followed the Wall Street Crash people began to realise that the USA's economic problems were not going to go away quickly. The crisis was so serious that it was called the **Depression**. Industry had produced too much, and now people could not afford to buy. If you look at source B you can see that more and more people lost their jobs. The families of the unemployed suffered as well. It has been estimated that about 40 million people (out of the USA's population of 120 million) were either unemployed or members of the family of an unemployed person.

The hire purchase system was badly damaged because large numbers of people couldn't afford to keep up the payments on their cars, radios and other goods. The companies which made these goods also suffered because too few people bought the goods. Things just seemed to get worse and worse.

Unemployed people had less to spend, so fewer people could afford to buy goods, and factories sacked even more workers. The textile industry was hit especially hard. Many people had to keep wearing their old clothes because they couldn't afford to buy new ones. 120 000 out of the state of New England's 280 000 textile workers lost their jobs in the early 1930s.

Even though people still needed to keep warm, they couldn't afford to buy coal. This meant that thousands of coal miners had to leave their jobs when prices fell. Some miners were so short of food that their children had to eat weeds and dandelions. Unemployed, shivering miners walked past mountains of coal on their way to the bread queue. People were desperate for work. Men who had previously been in well-paid jobs stood for hours on street corners, trying to earn a few cents by selling apples. Others walked around town

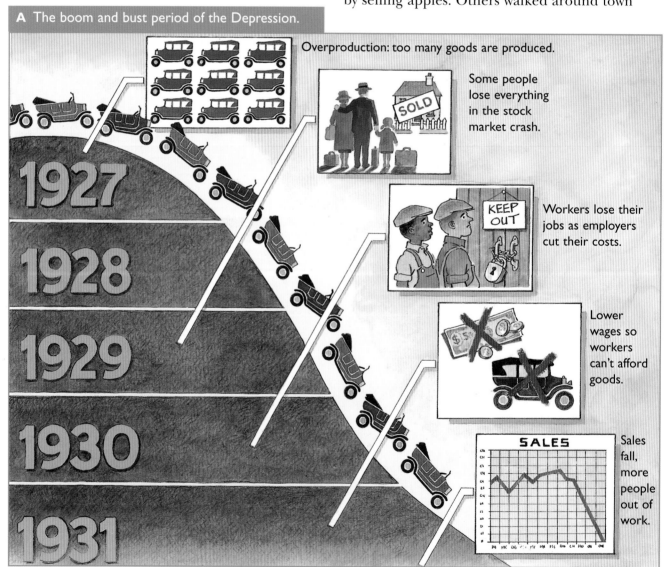

A The boom and bust period of the Depression.

Overproduction: too many goods are produced.

Some people lose everything in the stock market crash.

Workers lose their jobs as employers cut their costs.

Lower wages so workers can't afford goods.

Sales fall, more people out of work.

1927
1928
1929
1930
1931

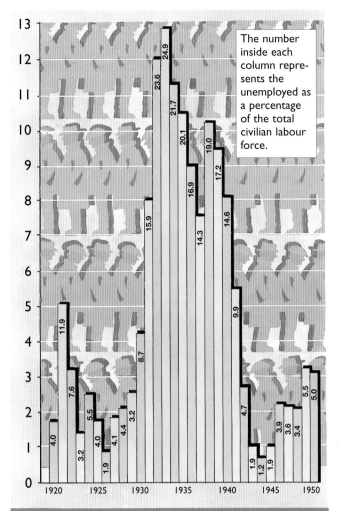

The number inside each column represents the unemployed as a percentage of the total civilian labour force.

B Changes in unemployment, 1920–50, showing the very high figures of the 1930s.

Year	National Income (in billions of dollars)
1929	87.8
1930	75.7
1931	59.7
1932	42.5
1933	40.2

C This table shows changes in national income from 1929 to 1933. The national income is the total value of goods produced and taxes collected by the government in one year.

D In March 1931 Henry Ford gave his opinion about the unemployment situation (quoted in *Brother Can You Spare A Dime?* by S Winslow, 1976).

The average man won't really do a day's work unless he is caught and cannot get out of it. There is plenty of work to do if people would do it.

E A social worker describes the life of an unemployed man from Chicago in the early 1930s (from *Case Studies of Unemployment* by M Elderton, 1931).

Every morning at six and sometimes earlier he was out looking for a job. He often only had a piece of bread for breakfast, and later there was not even enough of that for him and the kids, so he went without. This was in the winter. Once in a while he picked up a job shovelling snow. This helped with a little food but not nearly enough. The children began to lose weight and soon looked pale. His wife was not well and became more and more nervous with the strain. The gas was shut off, then the electricity. The grocery man, when he found that Pavlowski had no work, refused him credit.

carrying signs which said that they would try any job – even cleaning other people's shoes.

Bread queues

Because there was no unemployment pay, men had to queue up to get a bowl of soup and a piece of bread. These bread queues – sometimes 10 000 men long – became a familiar sight in most American cities. In 1932 the YMCA in one district of New York was giving away 12 000 free meals a day. Karl Monroe, an out-of-work newspaper reporter, remembered standing in bread queues. He was surprised to find that most of the men were skilled craftsmen who could not find work.

Private charities could not cope with such a huge crisis, so people had to find other ways of surviving. Men went to rubbish tips and spent hours scavenging for unwanted scraps of food. Others turned to begging in the streets. One woman remembered seeing 50 hungry men fighting like animals over a barrel of garbage which had been left at the back door of a restaurant.

1 Look at source B. How bad was the unemployment problem in the 1930s, compared with other decades?
2 Which was the worst year of the Depression? Use sources A on page 30, and B and C on page 33 in your answer.
3 Compare sources D and E.
   a) What differences do you notice in the way in which they describe how keen people were to get work?
   b) What reasons can you suggest for these differences? Think about the **provenance** of each source.

HOMELESSNESS

Some people lost their homes because they could no longer afford to keep up with the mortgage payments. Others, who rented their homes, also lost out and went to live in 'Hoovervilles'. These were shanty towns on the edge of cities all over the USA. They took their name from the President – the man whom more and more people began to blame for the misery in which they were living. Others became hoboes – they sneaked onto trains and moved from town to town in search of food. The problem was so serious that some communities employed armed guards to stop the hoboes from getting off the trains when they arrived in their areas.

Hoover and the Depression

President Hoover believed in self-help – people relying on their own efforts. He told the people that the USA had become a great country because its people had worked hard. Americans were rugged individuals – tough people who could sort out their problems without being told what to do by the government. His message was that the problem of unemployment would solve itself if people were patient for a little longer.

Hoover believed that economic freedom and political freedom were linked together. He thought that the USA would be in danger of becoming a socialist country if its government interfered with the work of businessmen. The President therefore refused to spend large amounts of government money on creating new jobs. He set up the President's Organisation for Unemployment Relief (POUR). The problem was that POUR did not spend government money on relieving unemployment – it only spent money donated by charities. This only made Hoover even more unpopular with the unemployed.

Hoover and the farmers

We saw on page 30 that many farmers did not share in the boom years of the 1920s. Foreign competition had caused prices to fall. Farmers who could no longer pay their rent had to leave their farms; often they moved to California in search of a better life. This problem became even worse during the Depression. At a time when many Americans were starving, Hoover angered people by telling farmers to grow fewer crops. The President thought that this would help prices to recover, but it only made him more unpopular.

Hoover and the banks

Banks which had lent too much money went bust. Between 1929 and 1932 more than 5000 banks closed down. Many Americans, therefore, lost their savings as well as their jobs. In 1931 Hoover finally decided that the government had to do more to help the economy recover. He set up the Reconstruction Finance Corporation, which lent

A Part of a 'Hooverville' in 1933. The shacks were made out of wood, boxes and any other materials that could be found on rubbish dumps. There were no proper toilets or washing facilities. Many of the people who lived in the Hoovervilles had only recently had decent jobs, before being thrown out of work by the Depression.

government money to help banks recover. His critics said that was not enough, and that much more should be done.

Rich people and the Depression

Large numbers of factories and shops were left empty because their owners had gone out of business. Some streets were quiet because fewer people could afford to run a car. Even some of the richer people had to make cutbacks. Some of them had to sack their servants. Rich wives, who had never done housework before, had to clean and cook. If you read source B, however, you can see that a number of richer Americans do not seem to have suffered very much during the Depression.

B A resident of Manhattan, one of New York's richest areas, remembers the Depression.

I don't think we ever mentioned the people on relief – never socially. Because I always had a theory – when you're out with friends, everything must be charming, and you don't allow the ugly.

There were no apple sellers – not in New York. Never, never. There were a few beggars. One day I saw this pathetic beggar whom I'd always felt sorry for. This Cadillac drove up. I'd just given him a quarter (25 cents) and it picked him up. There was a woman driving it. And I thought: well, if they can drive a Cadillac, they don't need my quarter.

I never saw one bread line, never in New York. If there were any, they were in Harlem or down in Greenwich Village. They were never in this section of town. The 'New Deal' meant absolutely nothing to me except higher taxation. The thirties was a glamorous, glittering moment.

Q

1 a) According to source B, how much suffering was there in New York during the Depression?
   b) How reliable is source B as evidence of the suffering in New York during the Depression?

2 a) Copy the diagram below to show the effects of the Depression on the USA. Fill in the empty boxes with effects of your own. Allow plenty of space because you may even need to add more boxes. Find information for your answer from pages 30 to 35.
   b) Give the diagram a key and shade in the economic effects.
   c) Use another colour to shade in the social effects.
   d) If you can find any other types of effects use other colours and add them to your key.
   e) Which do you think was the worst effect of the Depression on the USA? Why?

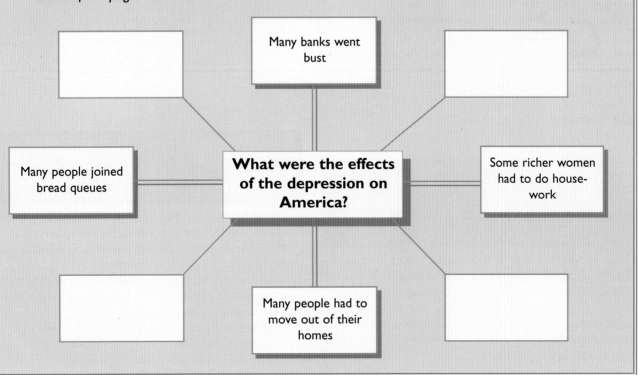

Many banks went bust

Many people joined bread queues

What were the effects of the depression on America?

Some richer women had to do housework

Many people had to move out of their homes

7

Who Was FD Roosevelt?

Although he came from a rich and privileged background, Roosevelt was elected President during the Depression. What made such a man a good leader at such a time? Why did Roosevelt win the 1932 election?

What kind of man was FD Roosevelt?

Franklin Delano Roosevelt (often known as FDR) was born in 1882. He came from a rich family in New York state. He lived in a mansion and went to one of the top schools in the country. In 1904 he gained a law degree from Harvard University. One year later he married his cousin, Eleanor Roosevelt, who was the niece of President Theodore Roosevelt. Franklin joined a New York law firm in 1907, but he was so rich that he did not have to work for a living. He could afford to become a politician and spend money on his election campaign for the New York state senate.

Not everyone was impressed with him when he entered politics. It was said that some people first voted for Roosevelt in 1910 because of the family name. The young Franklin seemed to be a serious man who was not very pleasant. Other members of the New York State Senate avoided Roosevelt.

But Roosevelt was soon successful as a politician and during the First World War became Assistant Secretary of State for the Navy.

Roosevelt became the only man in American history to be elected President four times, when he won the 1944 election.

A Frances Perkins, who later served in Roosevelt's government, first met him in 1910 when Roosevelt had just entered politics. Perkins remembers her early impressions of Roosevelt (from *The Roosevelt I Knew*, 1947).

No one who saw him in those years would have been likely to think of him as a potential President of the USA. He was not particularly charming (that came later). He rarely smiled and had an unfortunate habit of throwing his head up. This, combined with his great height, gave him the appearance of looking down his nose at most people.

What made Roosevelt a good leader?

In 1921, at the age of 39, Roosevelt was crippled with polio. Recovery was slow and tremendously hard work. He fought back and in 1928 became Governor of New York.

In 1932 Roosevelt stood against Hoover for President. He was a good speaker and somehow found the energy to make 15 speeches a day during the election. His election organiser, Jim Farley, said that Roosevelt was able to give the impression that he enjoyed meeting the people and shaking their hands. He had the 'common touch'.

The writer Raymond Moley followed Roosevelt's travels around the USA during the election. He explained that Roosevelt knew the people he waved to from the train had votes, but he waved to them mainly because he liked them. He was shocked by hunger and unemployment, and he wanted people to be as lucky as he had been. Roosevelt convinced people that he wanted to protect the Weak against the Strong.

He knew that he had to get the support of lots of people who wanted very different things. One way in which he did this was by keeping people guessing about what he was really thinking. He told the actor Orson Welles, 'You know Orson, you and I are the two best actors in America.'

Senator Huey Long said that when he went to talk to Roosevelt he would say, 'Fine, fine, fine.' But Joe Robinson (an opponent of Long) would see Roosevelt the next day and again he would say, 'Fine, fine, fine.' As Huey Long commented, 'Maybe he said "Fine" to everyone.'

B Roosevelt's wife Eleanor describes his fight against polio (from a letter written by Eleanor Roosevelt, quoted in *The Roosevelt Letters, Volume 2, 1905–1928*, edited by Elliott Roosevelt, 1948):

Perhaps the experience, above all others, which shaped my husband's character and gave him a strength and a depth he did not have as a young man was the long struggle with polio.

A strength of character was built up during those days which made him able to give complete confidence to the people of the nation when they needed it, so that when he said: 'The only thing we have to fear is fear itself,' they knew he believed it. He had lived through fear and come out successfully.

C One of his early advisers remembers Roosevelt's special qualities (from *Working with Roosevelt* by S Rosenman, 1952):

Having come to a decision, he would dismiss it from his mind as finished business. 'Once you've made a decision, there's no use worrying about whether you were right or wrong.' To the men who worked around him and who were prone to worry a great deal about the momentous decisions Roosevelt had to make, this was one of his most amazing qualities.

D His secretary remembers Roosevelt's qualities as a leader (from *FDR My Boss* by Grace Tully, 1949).

Roosevelt had great self confidence. He felt that he had been given a grand opportunity to do something about the problems which faced the nation. He felt sure of his own place in history. He had a will to take responsibility and to take decisions.

Joseph Zangara was an Italian bricklayer who fired five shots at Roosevelt on 15 February 1932 in Miami, Florida. The bullets missed Roosevelt but hit and killed Mayor Anton Cermak. Zangara went to the electric chair.

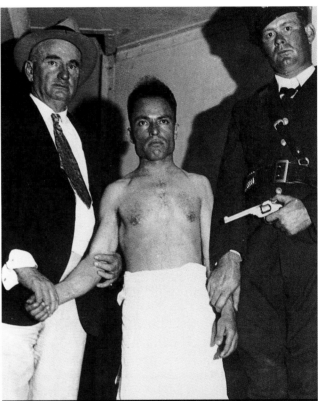

F Photograph of Joseph Zangara (centre) in police custody, 15 February 1932.

E A photograph of Roosevelt (pictured on the left). The photograph shows his leg braces. His disability was usually hidden from public view.

Q

1 Using the information in this unit make a time-line of important events in Roosevelt's life.
2 What do you think are the words that describe a good leader? Can you find any of these words in the sources in this unit?
3 What were Roosevelt's strengths as a leader? Give reasons for your answer.
4 a) What are the problems in using sources B, C and D to find out about Roosevelt's character? Think about the provenance of each source
   b) What other sources might help to give a more complete view of Roosevelt?

THE 1932 ELECTION

We saw in the last section that FD Roosevelt was a remarkable man. Did Roosevelt win the 1932 election because he was a good leader, or were other reasons more important?

Problems for President Hoover

At the beginning of 1932 there seemed to be no end in sight to the unemployment crisis. Millions of unemployed people were looking for food, shelter and work. Protest marches were held in many cities. In March 5000 unemployed workers marched on Henry Ford's production plant near Detroit. They were demanding work. Four men were killed when the marchers clashed with Ford Security guards and police.

Hoover's election campaign

Herbert Hoover was not a great public speaker. His speeches came across as rather boring and they did not contain any easy answers to the USA's problems. Hoover blamed the Depression on foreign bankers, but refused to take drastic action to end the crisis. He repeated his opinion that things would improve if people waited for the American economy to recover by itself. Hoover did not want to experiment with costly government schemes.

To make matters worse, Hoover's **Vice-President** predicted that good times were just around the corner. When the good times did not return people blamed Hoover. The President's name became a sign of bad times. We have already seen that the cardboard cities were called 'Hoovervilles'. A newspaper was nicknamed a 'Hoover blanket' and an unemployed man's empty pocket, turned inside out to show he had no money, was known as a 'Hoover flag'.

In the summer of 1932 the Bonus Army marchers, a group of unemployed men who had been soldiers in the First World War, went to Washington to ask the government to help them survive the Depression by paying their war pensions early. Hoover refused to help and ordered that they should be thrown out of the Hooverville shacks they were living in. The authorities used violence to destroy the Hoovervilles and a young child was killed. Pictures of the burning shacks were seen in the newspapers (see source D).

Roosevelt's election campaign

In June 1932 delegates of the Democratic Party met at their Convention in Chicago to choose their presidential candidate. The successful candidate would need the support of two-thirds of the delegates before he could be nominated. It was by no means certain that Roosevelt would get enough support. In the end he only got through because one of his rivals, a man called John Garner, agreed to stand aside and support Roosevelt for the good of the Democratic Party. Garner said, 'I'll do anything to see the Democrats win one more national election.' Garner had many supporters in the important states of California and Texas. They became Roosevelt supporters and in return Roosevelt gave Garner the job of Vice-President. This meant that his main rival in the Democratic Party was now on Roosevelt's side.

> John Garner agreed to be Roosevelt's Vice-President even though he knew that the Vice-President had very little power. Garner described the Vice-President's job as 'not worth a pitcher [jug] of warm spit'.

A Election poster issued by supporters of FD Roosevelt, 1932, also showing the Vice-Presidential candidate, John Garner.

B During his 1932 election campaign, Roosevelt made a speech in San Francisco promising action:

The country needs, and unless I mistake its mood, demands bold experiments. Above all, try something.

C The American historian, G B Tindall, criticised the attempts of the Hoover government to fight the Depression (from *America: A Narrative History*, 1992):

Not only did the policies of public officials help bring on economic collapse, but few public leaders acknowledged the crisis. They thought that the economy would cure itself. These ideas set limits to government action. Hoover was not ready to change, even to meet an emergency.

D Bonus Army shacks being burnt down after the 'battle' of Anacostia Flats, Washington, 1932.

Roosevelt accepted the nomination and told the Convention that he was going to do something new. He had deliberately broken with tradition and promised 'a **New Deal** for the American people'. He accused Hoover of failing to provide hope for the future. Roosevelt set off on a huge tour around the USA, meeting the people and showing them that he was tough enough to take on the job of President. Everywhere he went, Roosevelt's campaign tune of 'Happy Days Are Here Again' could be heard. He did not spell out in detail what this 'New Deal' would involve, he just convinced people that it would involve a better life. Roosevelt's cheerful smile was seen in photographs which appeared in the newspapers. People cheered when Roosevelt promised to end prohibition. Roosevelt gave the impression that he was confident about the USA's future.

1 What do you think was clever about the way Roosevelt fought his election campaign?
2 What mistakes to you think Hoover made in his election campaign?
3 What does source A suggest about one possible reason for Roosevelt's victory in the 1932 election?
4 What impact to you think the attack on the Bonus Army had on Hoover's election chances?
5 'The Wall Street Crash cost Hoover the 1932 election.' How far do you agree with this interpretation of Roosevelt's victory in the 1932 election? (Remember to consider other possible reasons in addition to the Wall Street Crash.)

8

The New Deal

What did Roosevelt's promised New Deal actually involve? Who opposed the New Deal and why?

The hundred days

During his first **hundred days** as President, FD Roosevelt was a very busy man. He put forward many new ideas which he hoped would help revive the American economy. His aims were:

- to help industry, business and farming recover from the Depression;
- to cut unemployment and provide jobs for people;
- to provide relief for those who had been hardest hit by the Depression.

Hoover had told the voters to wait for the economic recovery to happen. Roosevelt decided that he would not wait. He promised a 'New Deal' for the American people. As a result the government passed the so-called **Alphabet Laws** which set up new agencies to plan and carry out the economic recovery. Some of these new agencies came to be known by their initials. See pages 42 to 43 for information about their work.

Before he could pass the new laws Roosevelt had to sort out the banking emergency. Roosevelt had become President at a time of crisis. People

To get help to ordinary people as quickly as possible the government made an immediate grant of $500 million available through a brand new agency, the Federal Emergency Relief Administration. Harry Hopkins was put in charge of the agency. During his first morning in office he gave away $5 million.

had lost confidence in their banks, because they thought the banks would go bust and their savings would be lost. People queued up to take their money out of the banks. Roosevelt solved the problem by declaring a 'bank holiday'. His Emergency Banking Act was passed on 5 March 1933. It ordered that banks be closed for a time. The badly run banks stayed shut and government money helped the better banks to re-open. People put their money back into the banks and confidence began to return.

In June 1933 a plan was agreed to help industry recover. The plan was known as the National Industrial Recovery Act. It set up a job creation agency called the Public Works Administration (PWA), and an organisation called the National Recovery Administration (NRA). The NRA was an organisation which tried to get bosses and workers together to draw up codes or rules by which their industries should be run. These would lay down basic standards about pay and hours to be worked. Firms which obeyed the code could display the Blue Eagle badge of the NRA. We shall see on page 46 that many people were opposed to the NRA. Roosevelt, however, claimed that the NRA had been good for the USA. It had helped stop child labour and had introduced the idea of consumers' rights, trade union rights and the minimum wage.

The Public Works Administration (PWA)

This organised large building projects, such as the construction of dams and bridges. The PWA also organised the clearance of old slum housing and the building of new blocks of flats. Harold Ickes was in charge of spending over $6 billion on public works. The PWA built over a third of America's hospitals as well as 1000 airports and 40 000 schools.

1932 election	(Numbers in millions)
FD Roosevelt (Democrat Party)	23.0
Herbert Hoover (Republican Party)	15.0
Norman Thomas (Socialist Party)	0.8
William Foster (Communist Party))	0.1
1936 election	
FD Roosevelt (Democrat)	27.7
Alfred Landon (Republican)	16.6
Lemke (Union)	0.8
Norman Thomas (Socialist)	0.1
Browder (Communist)	0.08

A These figures show the number of votes each candidate received in the 1932 and 1936 presidential elections. Each time Roosevelt won by a very large margin.

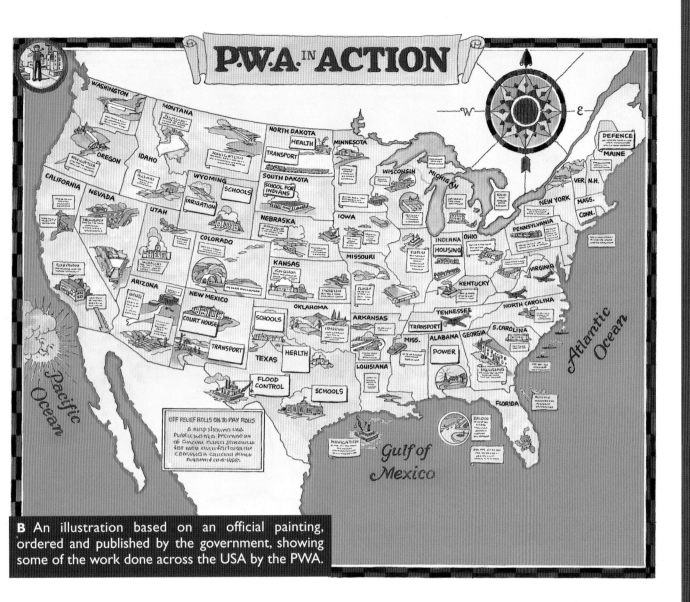

B An illustration based on an official painting, ordered and published by the government, showing some of the work done across the USA by the PWA.

1 Look carefully at source B. Copy and complete the chart to show the work of the PWA in particular states. The first one has been done for you.

State	Work done by the PWA
1 Wyoming	Irrigation, schools
2 Alabama	
3 North Dakota	
4 Maine	
5 Indiana	
6 Texas	
7 Tennessee	
8 New Mexico	
9 South Dakota	

2 a) Draw bar charts from source A to show the election results of 1932 and 1936.

  b) What can you tell from source A about Roosevelt's popularity with the American voters? Back up your answer with figures from the source.

3 a) What point do you think is being made in source B about the work of the PWA? Give examples from the illustration to support your answer.

  b) How reliable is source B as evidence of the work of the PWA? Use the source text and its provenance to give reasons for your answer.

4 Do the unemployment figures on page 33 help you understand the election results shown in source A? Explain your answer.

ROOSEVELT AND THE ALPHABET LAWS

These illustrations give you an introduction to some of the many laws passed by Roosevelt's government during the New Deal. The page numbers tell you about other places in the book where you can find out more about these laws.

3 The FHA (Federal Housing Administration), 1934. It gave ordinary families a better chance of buying their own homes. The government gave help with mortgages. The FHA helped house-buyers by making sure that they did not have to put down such a large deposit on a house as in previous years. They were also given longer to pay back the mortgage.

1 The HOLC (Home Owners Loan Corporation). People who couldn't keep up with their mortgage payments were helped by the HOLC.

4 The TVA (Tennessee Valley Authority), 1933. The TVA helped farmers experiment with new farming methods. It supervised the building of dams and lakes in an area which covered seven American states. The TVA helped stop flooding and soil erosion and brought electricity and new industries to one of the poorest parts of the country. (See page 50.)

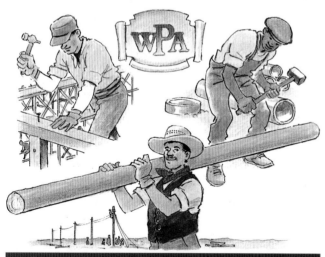

2 The WPA (Works Progress Administration), 1935. It aimed to give unemployed people work which would be useful to the local community. They built many new schools and thousands of kilometres of new roads. Unemployed artists were hired to paint pictures on the walls of the new schools and post offices. Between 1935 and 1942 the WPA is thought to have provided about eight million jobs.

5 The AAA (Agricultural Adjustment Administration), 1933. Many farmers had seen such a huge fall in the prices of their products that they could no longer afford to pay their rent. The AAA gave farmers money to buy machinery and fertilisers. They also cut production and killed animals to drive up prices. They did this because goods which are in short supply tend to rise in price. This would boost the farmer's income. (See page 48.)

6 The CCC (Civilian Conservation Corps). Unemployed young Americans were given food and lived in special camps. They were paid a dollar a day to work in the forests. They planted trees and restocked rivers with fish. About 2.5 million found work with the CCC.

7 In 1935 President Roosevelt introduced the National Labour Act, which allowed workers to form trade unions. There were strikes and violence when employers such as Henry Ford sacked people who tried to join unions and ask for higher wages.

9 The Fair Labor Standards Act, 1938.
This brought pay rises and shorter hours of work for thousands of Americans, because it laid down basic minimum wages and maximum hours of work.

8 The Social Security Act, 1935.
This gave government pensions to old, sick and disabled people who couldn't provide for themselves. It also introduced the USA's first national system of unemployment benefit. The money came from special taxes paid by workers and employers. (See pages 56–57.)

1 Look at the changes shown in the illustrations above.
  a) Choose three which you think made Roosevelt more popular in the 1930s.
  b) Explain why they made him more popular.
2 Did everyone benefit from the changes shown in the illustrations? Give reasons for your answer.
3 Which of the changes shown in the illustrations do you think was the most important in the long run:
  a) in helping the economy to recover;
  b) in improving people's rights?

OPPOSITION

Roosevelt and the Republicans

No sooner had the New Deal begun than the Republicans criticised Roosevelt. They said that Roosevelt was trying to bribe the American people into voting for him with his job creation schemes. Republicans felt that Americans could not afford all this money that Roosevelt was spending.

The previous President, Herbert Hoover, also accused Roosevelt of wasting government money. We have seen that Hoover believed in self-help. He thought that government should not spend taxpayers' money on employment schemes. People should provide for themselves, he thought, otherwise they would go 'soft' and not work hard enough.

Huey Long

It was not just the Republicans who opposed Roosevelt. He also faced criticism from inside the Democratic Party.

Huey Long was just such a critic of Roosevelt. Long was a lawyer who became a successful politician. He saw himself as the defender of poor white people in the South and made speeches in which he criticised the power of big business.

In 1928 Long was elected Governor of Louisiana. His policy of spending money on schools and roads was popular. He had reduced unemployment in Louisiana. In 1930 he was elected to the Senate. He promised that if he were President he would share out the nation's income more fairly. He would take away the fortunes of people who had more than $3 million and give poorer Americans a lump sum of $5000.

His 'Share Our Wealth' scheme was first put forward in 1932 and clubs were formed in many parts of the USA. In 1935 he claimed that there were 27 431 'Share Our Wealth' clubs with a membership of 7.5 million Americans. Long said that every adult should have a minimum wage of $2000 a year. About half of the American people earned less than that. He said that he would grant pensions to old people, reduce the length of the working week and pay the war veterans' bonuses. He also claimed that he would be able to provide a college education for every qualified student. Long made many enemies and was assassinated in 1935. The 'Share Our Wealth' movement died with him.

"Mother Wilfred wrote a bad word!"

A The wealthy business classes hated Roosevelt's New Deal and they hated him. They believed his policies threatened their profits. There must have been many upper-class families where the word 'Roosevelt' was indeed a dirty word, as this cartoon suggests.

The rich

Roosevelt faced opposition from business leaders. Previous Presidents had taken advice from rich businessmen and tried to create conditions in which their businesses would make big profits. With more than ten million Americans still unemployed in 1934, Roosevelt felt that bold economic policies were needed. Rich businessmen wanted less government action. They thought that the 'business of America is business' and that the government ought not to interfere in the economy. Roosevelt was afraid that if he did not act quickly then the crisis would get even worse and the economy would not recover. When the President pressed on with his Alphabet Laws he found that rich businessmen criticised him for meddling in their work.

Very rich people disliked the New Deal because they had to pay higher taxes which were needed to help finance it. In April 1936 a journalist wrote that members of the upper classes 'frankly hate Franklin Roosevelt'. They called him a 'traitor to his class'. In 1934 a few millionaires organised a Liberty League to defend private wealth and business profits.

The Liberty League was made up of businessmen and politicians from both major political parties. The Liberty Leaguers spent large sums of money on their campaign of opposition to Roosevelt and his New Deal. They claimed that the USA had been a great nation but that Roosevelt was a threat to the country's freedom. The Liberty Leaguers accused Roosevelt of trying to turn the USA into a totalitarian government, like Nazi German or fascist Italy, in which the government tried to take control over the lives of the people. According to the Liberty League, it was the businessmen who had made the USA great, because they had shown what could be achieved if free men were allowed to work hard and build a dream. They saw Roosevelt as a threat to the American way of life.

The Liberty League were also worried by New Deal policies which they thought had been designed to give more rights to workers. Businessmen feared that this might damage the economy and cost them money.

Workers

Some workers supported Roosevelt because they thought his government was standing up to the bosses and looking after the rights of ordinary working people. Other workers felt that the government could have done more to protect and strengthen the trade unions – particularly when unions went on strike. Roosevelt's Secretary for Labor remembered that there 'were many things about trade unions that Roosevelt never fully understood'. He was afraid of a class struggle between rich and poor, so he avoided giving too much support to striking workers.

Farm workers also criticised the New Deal. In the Southern states poor **sharecroppers** – both black and white – formed the Southern Tenant Farmers' Union. They were angry that rich landlords were getting most of the money given by the government's Agricultural Adjustment Act to help farmers. Their protests were crushed by the landlords and the government did nothing to help.

B One of Roosevelt's most bitter critics was Father Coughlin, a Catholic priest, who gave talks on the radio. He founded the *National Union for Social Justice.* He blamed some of the country's problems on the Jews, and called the New Deal the 'Jew Deal'. Ten million Americans tuned in to hear him blame Roosevelt for America's problems. This is an extract from one of his radio talks, quoted in the *New York Times,* 17 July 1936:

Roosevelt is the great betrayer and liar. He promised to drive the money changers from the temple and succeeded in driving the farmers from their homes. He has built up the greatest debt in all history, $35 billion, which he allowed the bankers to spend, that you and your children shall repay with seventy billion hours of labour to farms, to factories and to places of business. Seven seconds to coin the money and seventy billion hours to pay it back!

C In the year he was assassinated, 1935, Huey Long, the Democratic Senator from Louisiana, made a speech in Congress highly critical of the government:

While millions have starved, while babies have cried and died for milk, while people have begged for meat and bread, Mr Roosevelt's government has sailed merrily along, plowing under and destroying the things to eat and to wear.

And now it is with PWAs, NRAs, AAAs and every other flimsy combination that the country finds its affairs and business tangled to where no one can recognise it. More men are now out of work than ever; the debt of the United States has gone up another $10 billion. There is starvation; there is homelessness; there is misery on every hand and in every corner.

1 Why do you think Huey Long had:
   a) lots of supporters;
   b) powerful enemies?
2 What similarities do you notice in the criticisms of Roosevelt in sources B and C?
3 How might a supporter of Roosevelt have replied to the criticisms in sources B and C?
4 The modern historian, Geoffrey Hodgson, said that Roosevelt's greatest achievement was 'to raise people's hopes again, to convince them something was at last being done to help'. What reasons can you give to explain why this interpretation is so different from Father Coughlin's view in source B?

OTHER OPPONENTS

Landon's supporters

In 1936 Roosevelt's first four-year term as President was ending and he decided to run for re-election. His main rival was the Republican candidate, Alfred Landon. Supporters of Landon accused Roosevelt of reckless spending. They also accused him of trying to be too powerful – like a dictator. Landon's supporters said that Roosevelt was trying to make the American people slaves of an all-powerful state. One claimed that we had to turn back many centuries 'to find so great a power over the lives of millions of men lodged in the hands of a single person'. The results of the election can be seen in source A.

Businessmen

Many businessmen were opponents of the New Deal because they felt that it gave too much power to the workers. The NRA (National Recovery Administration), for example, allowed workers collective bargaining in negotiations for better pay and conditions. In 1934 and 1935 there were a number of bitter industrial disputes. Sometimes workers were locked out of their factories until they agreed to accept lower wages or worse conditions. On other occasions strikes were broken up violently. Industrialists suspected that Roosevelt sympathised with the workers.

Businessmen tended to dislike the New Deal for other reasons too. They did not like the many New Deal laws which interfered with their business. These laws had brought about important changes – such as the eight-hour day, minimum wages and the ending of child labour in the coal mines. Some people feared that Roosevelt was turning the USA into a socialist country with all his government's rules and regulations. Roosevelt, of course, denied that he was a socialist, but found that he had to keep defending his government against the charge that it was getting too inefficient and interfering too much in the lives of the people. In 1932 there were 500 000 American civil servants. By 1939 the number had risen to 920 000. Source B shows some of these fears about government 'red tape'.

Roosevelt thought that business was not just about making big profits – it was also about looking after the welfare of the country. Many businessmen didn't see things like that. They found it more difficult to relate to Roosevelt, who had been born into a rich family, than to the previous President, Herbert Hoover, who had

become a self-made millionaire. He and Coolidge believed that 'the business of America is business'. This made much more sense to bosses than Roosevelt's New Deal.

Candidate	Party	Number of votes (in millions)	States won
Roosevelt	**Democratic**	27.7	46
Landon	**Republican**	16.6	2
Lemke	**Union**	0.8	0

A Results of the 1936 Presidential election.

B Cartoon from the magazine *Vanity Fair*, 1935, showing **Uncle Sam** (representing the USA) tied down. Each of the ropes stands for part of the New Deal. The cartoon is based on the story of *Gulliver's Travels*, in which Captain Gulliver was tied up by tiny people from Lilliput.

The Supreme Court

If you look at the diagram on page 2 you can see that the Supreme Court is powerful because it can decide whether an Act passed by Congress is legal. In 1935 and 1936 the Supreme Court decided New

C 'Nine Old Men', an American cartoon depicting the elderly judges in the Supreme Court, May, 1937.

Deal laws such as the Agricultural Adjustment Administration and the National Industrial Recovery Act broke the Constitution. This meant that these laws could not be carried out, so Roosevelt had to drop them.

Roosevelt was angry that part of his New Deal had been blocked. He thought that some of the judges on the Supreme Court were supporters of the Republicans – whereas they were supposed to be neutral. Some of the judges were old men and Roosevelt felt that they should be made to retire at 70. Roosevelt thought that he had enough support from the people (source A) to 'take on' the Supreme Court.

He asked Congress to let him replace the older judges with up to six younger judges of his choice. Congress angrily refused. Roosevelt's critics said that he was trying to be a dictator (someone like Hitler or Stalin) and refused to allow him the power to interfere with the Supreme Court. Roosevelt had to abandon his plans and was forced instead to co-operate with the Supreme Court.

1 Copy the chart and complete it to show who opposed Roosevelt's New Deal and why.

People	Reason for opposition
Republicans	They said Roosevelt was trying to buy votes, and the USA couldn't afford it.
Herbert Hoover	
Huey Long	
Father Coughlin	

2 Look at source B.
   a) What can you see in the cartoon to suggest that it is about the USA?

   b) Using pages 42–43 explain what any two of the sets of initials on the ropes stand for.

   c) Do you think the cartoon was drawn by a supporter or an opponent of the New Deal? Explain your answer.

3 Look at source C. Carefully describe the faces of the Supreme Court judges. What do you think the cartoonist is trying to 'say' about the Supreme Court?

4 How much opposition was there to Roosevelt's New Deal? Study source A and the rest of the information and sources in this unit before giving your answer.

5 What does the story of Roosevelt and the Supreme Court tell us about the power of the President?

9

The New Deal – Winners and Losers

On balance, were there more winners or losers under Roosevelt's New Deal? How successful were the schemes, such as the Tennessee Valley Authority, set up to help the losers? What about women and the various minority groups – did they find the New Deal a fair deal?

B A map showing the Dust Bowl states, where the land was badly eroded through overcropping. Drought and dust storms made conditions even harder here for many farmers during the Depression.

Change usually affects different people in different ways. Historians use the word *progress* to describe changes for the better – and the word *regress* to describe changes for the worse. Sometimes, of course, things don't really change very much – and in that case historians use the word *continuity*.

This unit tries to draw up a 'balance sheet' for the New Deal by finding out how it affected different groups of American people, and by asking who gained and who lost from it.

How much help did the New Deal give to Dust Bowl farmers?

Many farmers had suffered in the 1920s because prices for their goods were low. Farmers tried to

A A Missouri family who had been forced to leave their farm are photographed with all their possessions on the way to the California peafields.

earn more money by growing more crops, but this only made things worse because the prices fell even lower. In some places wheat was left to rot because it did not pay to harvest it.

Roosevelt knew that about a third of American voters depended on farming for their living. He tried to help the farmers with his Agricultural Adjustment Act (the AAA). He hoped that farm prices would go up again if farmers produced less. This would eventually mean that farmers would start making profits again. In the meantime the farmers needed help. Under the AAA the government gave the farmers money to help them survive. Six million pigs were slaughtered to try and force up the price of pork.

Hungry farmers who had lost their homes, their farms and their jobs in the **Dust Bowl** (see source B) could not understand why animals were being killed and crops left to rot. The historian A J Badger has written that between 1932 and 1936 the AAA helped raise farmers' income by 50 per cent. He thought that farmers' debts had been cut by a billion dollars. But the AAA helped the richer farmers who owned more land and could make use of tractors and other machines on their farms. The tenant farmers, who rented small strips of land and could not afford new machinery suffered. More than three million people from the Dust Bowl states had to leave their farms and work in other states.

C An official government report looks at the problems farmers faced in 1935 (from *Farmers on Relief and Rehabilitation*, 1935).

In many parts of the country, farmers have been attempting for years to cultivate soil which was never suitable for farming. Such soil has given them only the barest living and made it impossible for them to better their condition.

Warnings of soil erosion have been heard in many areas for years, but these have been ignored by farmers who were too eager for immediate results to care about the future. Other farmers could not afford the outlay necessary to prevent erosion, or had such limited acreages that they had no choice but to use their land to the full, regardless of the danger of overcropping. In 1934 the National Resources Board reported that the usefulness for farming of 35 million acres had been completely destroyed, that the topsoil was nearly or entirely removed from another 125 million acres, and that destruction had begun on another 100 million acres.

When the Depression brought these conditions to a climax, acreage was sharply reduced, and farmers were evicted from the land. With no resources of any kind … large numbers of families were left stranded, bewildered and helpless.

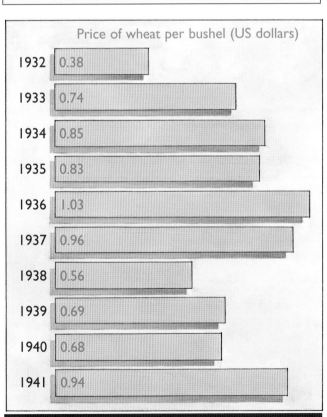

Price of wheat per bushel (US dollars)

Year	Price
1932	0.38
1933	0.74
1934	0.85
1935	0.83
1936	1.03
1937	0.96
1938	0.56
1939	0.69
1940	0.68
1941	0.94

D Changes in the price of wheat per bushel (in dollars). A high price for wheat meant that the farmers who grew it were doing well. The lower the price the less money they got.

E The novelist John Steinbeck tells the story of poor tenant farmers who were forced to leave their cottonfields and to travel to California in search of work. In this extract from *The Grapes of Wrath* (1939) the tenant farmers (who rent the land) are worried that the landowners will make them leave the land. The people in the story are fictional characters but they were based on people Steinbeck met when he lived with tenant farmers as part of his research for the book.

The owners of the land came on to the land … in closed cars, and they felt the earth with their dry fingers. The tenants, from their sun-beaten dooryards watched uneasily … And at last the owner men sat in their cars to talk out of the windows … You know the land is poor, you've scrabbed it long enough, God knows.

The squatting tenant men nodded and wondered and drew figures in the dust, and yes, they knew, God knows. If only the dust wouldn't fly. If the top would only stay on the soil, it might not be so bad.

The owner men went on leading to their point: you know the land's getting poorer. You know what cotton does to the land: robs it, sucks the blood out of it.

The squatting men looked down again. What do you want us to do? We can't take less share of the crop, we're half starved now. The kids are hungry all the time. We got no clothes, torn an' ragged …

At last the owner men came to the point. The tenant system won't work any more. One man on a tractor can take the place of twelve or fourteen families. Pay him a wage and take all the crop. We have to do it.

Q

1 Look at source A. How can you tell that the people in the photograph are poor?
2 Look at source B. Make a list of states which had been severely affected by the Dust Bowl and dust storms.
3 If you wanted to show that the New Deal was not very helpful for farmers, how would you use sources C and D?
4 Compare the way sources C and E describe life for farmers. What similarities do you notice?
5 Source E is an extract from a novel. Does that mean it is not useful to the historian of farming in 1930s America? Explain your answer. (Clue: think about the provenance of the source.)
6 'The New Deal did little to help farmers.' Using sources A to E and your own knowledge explain whether you agree or disagree with this interpretation.

CASE STUDY: HOW SUCCESSFUL WAS THE TENNESSEE VALLEY AUTHORITY (TVA)?

On 10 April 1933 President Roosevelt asked Congress to set up a new planning authority in one region of the USA – the area around the Tennessee River. This area, seen in source A, stretched over seven states and covered over 100 000 square kilometres. It was one of the poorest parts of the country:

- only three out of every 100 of its farms had electricity;
- levels of malaria and vitamin deficiency disease were very high;
- average income was only 40 per cent of the national average;
- many of its farmers were in debt; and
- there wasn't much manufacturing industry.

A Map showing parts of the USA covered by the Tennessee Valley Authority (TVA).

The TVA is thought to have been the USA's first experiment in regional development. It became the model for similar schemes in other parts of the world. President Roosevelt said that the TVA should aim to benefit the people of the area, and of the country as a whole. This was to be done by producing plans for the development of the area,

The peasant farmers used primitive farming methods. They cut down trees but they failed to use fertilisers. The soil lost its fertility and large amounts of it were simply washed away. The erosion was appalling. Looking at the dirty Tennessee River I was told that there were men still living who remembered it as a clear blue stream. Here under my eyes was the basic productivity being stripped from a vast area and hurried along to sterile waste in the sea.

including building dams, flood control, generating electricity, planting trees to stop soil erosion, and introducing better farming methods.

All this was to be done by involving ordinary people in the planning so that they would be taking part in making decisions which affected their own future. Roosevelt called it a 'democratic partnership'. The TVA worked by getting the co-operation of local land-grant colleges. These were organisations which helped plan the way in which the area around the river would be used. Farmers took part in these land-grant colleges.

Two views about how successful the TVA was are given in sources C and D.

The visitor to the TVA area in the 1960s would have found a much changed place from that of the early 1930s. Most people no longer worked in

You can see the change best of all if you have flown down the valley as I have done so frequently during these past ten years. From 5000 feet the great change is unmistakable … you can see the grey dams, and the river now deep blue, no longer red and murky with its hoard of soil washed from the eroding land.

And marching toward every point on the horizon you can see the steel crisscross of electric transmission towers. An area about the size of England and Scotland, with a population of about 4.5 million people: this is the river system the dams control and have put to work for the people.

In ten years the dams TVA has built have made this region the second largest producer of power in the United States. In 1944 the system will produce nearly half as much electricity as the utilities of the entire country produced in 1914. A kilowatt hour of electricity is a modern slave, working tirelessly for men.

D A sociologist interviewed local farmers as part of his special study of the way in which the TVA worked (from *TVA and the Grass Roots* by P Selznick, 1966).

The land-grant colleges were closely tied to the interests of the richer farmers. They had little or nothing to do with the poor, mainly black tenant farmers. The services offered by the TVA – advice on new farming developments, fertilisers and marketing – were monopolised by the richer, white farmers.

The TVA originally planned to develop the land around the newly built reservoirs for public use. However the richer farmers strongly opposed this policy because they wanted to keep control of the land. It was much more valuable because its soil had been enriched by the reservoirs. Under pressure from the richer farmers the TVA changed its policy and allowed the land to remain in private ownership. The TVA survived, but in doing so, it lost all claim to be democratic.

The public, whose taxes had paid for the reservoirs, failed to benefit either from the areas around the reservoirs or from the rising land prices.

E Two photographs showing, above, badly eroded land in the Tennessee Valley in the early 1930s, and below, farmland in the Tennessee Valley after treatment by TVA experts.

agriculture. Different types of jobs had been created in the region. The new industries include chemicals, food-processing plants, paper mills, an atomic energy centre and car factories. By the 1960s the TVA region had a greater share of manufacturing jobs than the national average.

Wages were rising – from 40 per cent of the national average in the 1930s, to 70 per cent by the early 1960s. Fewer farmers were having to leave the area.

Demand for electricity continued to grow. The hydroelectric dams of the 1930s supplied some of the necessary power, and the rest was supplied in the next 50 years by coal-powered and nuclear-powered systems which were also built in the TVA area. By 1980 the TVA had become the largest single consumer of coal in the USA.

Eventually 33 large dams were built alongside the Tennessee River. Longer stretches of the river are open to shipping. Now that the flow of the river has been controlled, it has become easier to stamp out malaria, and therefore make the local population healthier.

New housing and watersports facilities have been built alongside the lakes which were created as part of the TVA plans. Conservation policies have resulted in the reforestation of over a quarter of a million acres of the Tennessee Valley. The area is green again. Soil erosion has been tackled. There are twice as many trees as there were in the 1930s.

1 Look at source A. List the seven states of the TVA.
2 Use source B and the information in this unit to make a list of problems faced by farmers of the TVA in 1933.
3 Compare the way in which sources C and D explain the success of the TVA.
   a) What differences do you notice?
   b) What reasons can you suggest for these differences?
4 Look at pages 48–51. What changes took place in farming in the TVA area? Make a list.
5 Did the changes take place quickly or slowly?
6 Did everybody benefit from these changes? Explain your answer.
7 How useful are photographs such as those seen in source E as evidence of the success of the TVA?

WOMEN WORKERS AND THE NEW DEAL

There were no programmes in the New Deal which were directed only at women. This of course doesn't necessarily mean that the New Deal did nothing for women. Women were included in those who benefited from the TVA (page 50), the NRA (page 40) and Social Security (page 43).

Did the New Deal bring progress for women workers? We saw on page 8 that in the 1920s many employers discriminated against women. In the 1930s more than 75 per cent of American school boards refused to employ wives. The civil service only allowed one member of a family to work for them – usually it was the wife who gave way to the husband. Therefore many women who worked in the 1920s lost their jobs in the 1930s. Many of those who had been housewives in the 1920s remained housewives during the New Deal years.

Source A gives you an idea of how quickly the number of women workers was growing. The average yearly salary for a woman in 1937 was $525 a year, compared with $1027 for a

> An opinion poll found that 82 per cent of Americans did not approve of wives going out to work. 75 per cent of the women in the opinion poll agreed.

man. 2.75 million people were involved in the Civilian Conservation Corps (page 43), but only 8000 of them were women.

FD Roosevelt was not known as a great supporter of women's rights, but he was a clever politician and he knew that after 1920 women made up more than half of the voters. He encouraged women to take part in politics. He appointed women to important jobs. Mary Rumsey, for example, was given an important job in the running of the NRA. Women were appointed federal judges and ambassadors for the first time. In 1934 the first women were elected to the Senate and to the **House of Representatives**. The historian Robert Divine has argued that government employment was one of the few areas in which working women made progress in the 1930s.

A biography of Eleanor Roosevelt

Eleanor Roosevelt married FDR in 1905. She devoted her time to looking after her husband and raising their family. When Franklin was disabled with polio in 1921 Eleanor worked hard to help him return to politics. She went to meetings of groups such as the League of Women's Voters and got used to making speeches. She told an audience in 1928 that it was important to 'bring government closer to the people'.

When Roosevelt became President his wife did not just keep quiet and stay out of politics. Eleanor had a huge amount of energy and toured the country, talking to different groups of poor, 'forgotten' Americans. She wanted a fairer and more equal society. She urged the WPA to create more jobs for women. She supported the Women's Trade Union League in its fight for equal pay for equal work. Some of her press conferences were for female journalists only – so that she could help more women break into that profession. Eleanor Roosevelt wrote a newspaper column 'My Day' in which she commented on women's issues. Her main concern was for social justice – for all groups, whether they were women, black people, Mexican immigrants or Native Americans.

Sometimes her opinions did not fit in with government policy. Her husband needed the support of politicians from the Southern states –

> During the New Deal a Chicago civic group declared that working women 'are holding jobs that rightfully belong to the God-intended providers of the households' – the men!

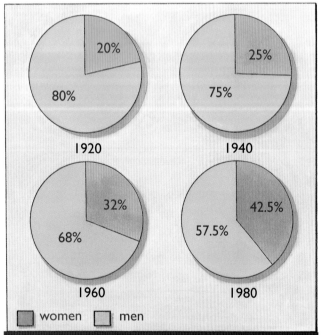

A These pie charts show the percentages of women and men in the United States labour force from 1920–80 (1960 and 1980 are provided as comparisons to the first part of the 20th century).

20%
80%
1920

25%
75%
1940

32%
68%
1960

42.5%
57.5%
1980

☐ women ☐ men

where there was opposition to civil rights for black people. Eleanor Roosevelt, therefore, could show more support for the rights of women and black people than her husband could. One of Franklin's advisers was so annoyed with Mrs Roosevelt's involvement in politics that he wrote: 'I wish Mrs Roosevelt would stick to her knitting.'

B This photograph shows Frances Perkins, as Secretary of State for Labour, greeting Clement Attlee on his arrival in the USA. When she was chosen by Roosevelt to be his Secretary of State for Labour, Frances Perkins became the first ever female cabinet member. She played an important part in government policies on relief, labour and welfare.

She did not stick to her knitting. She travelled across the country, even going down coal mines, reporting back to FDR on what was wrong with the USA. She did not miss a chance to speak up for women and other 'forgotten people'.

C The historian T K Hareven assesses the importance of Eleanor Roosevelt (from *Eleanor Roosevelt: An American Conscience*, 1968).

Franklin listened patiently to Eleanor's pleas on behalf of the downtrodden and heard views he would not have encountered otherwise from labour leaders and social workers whom she had talked to – but he did not take her into his political confidence more than anyone else, which is to say very little. Eleanor was immensely energetic, patient and gracious, deeply humanitarian and often naive, but thoroughly determined; she was, in short, the conscience of the New Deal. After FDR's death she became an international stateswoman in her own right. By any standard she was one of the great women of this century.

D Eleanor Roosevelt visits an African American nursery school run by the WPA in Des Moines, Iowa.

Q

1 Look at source A.
   a) Copy the charts or draw your own diagrams to show the same information.
   b) Between which years was the number of women workers growing most quickly:
      (i) 1920–40, (ii) 1940–60 or
      (iii) 1960–80? Give the figures in your answer.
2 How much progress did the New Deal bring for women? Begin by copying and completing the chart opposite (it has been started for you). Use the text and sources in this unit to help you. The completed table should then help you to write your answer.

Changes for the better	Things which didn't change much.
Women were appointed judges	Over 75 per cent of school boards refused to hire wives.

3 How useful are photographs in sources B and D as evidence to the historian of women's rights during the New Deal?
4 Why do you think that Eleanor Roosevelt played such an important part in the struggle for women's rights in the 1930s?

A Fair Deal For Minority Groups?

Black people and the New Deal

We saw on page 10 that in the 1920s black people suffered discrimination from the Jim Crow laws. Even black people who had moved to the Northern cities were treated as second class citizens. Eleanor Roosevelt gave her husband detailed reports about the suffering of the black people. She asked him to support a law against lynching. FDR refused because he did not want to upset politicians from the Southern states. He needed their support for other New Deal laws.

Most local Jim Crow laws were still in force during the New Deal. The Ku Klux Klan was allowed to continue with its activities. Only one civil rights law was passed by Roosevelt's government – to make discrimination against black employees in the defence industries illegal. The armed forces were still segregated. Black and white soldiers fought and died for their country – but in segregated units.

Black people were given leading government jobs. Mary McLeod Bethune, for example, gained a top job in the National Youth Administration (NYA). She helped organise training grants for high school students who were looking for work.

Voting figures show that black people voted for Roosevelt and helped him to be re-elected. In 1936 about 75 per cent of black people who voted are thought to have supported Roosevelt's Democratic party.

In 1933 white jobless demonstrators in Atlanta chanted: 'No jobs for Niggers until every white man has a job.'

Times were hard for black families during the New Deal. By 1933 more than 50 per cent of black workers in cities were unemployed. Poor black farmers were hit very hard by the fall in the price of cotton from 18 to six cents a pound. This did not bring in enough money to feed a family properly. The National Recovery Administration (NRA) allowed employers to pay black people less than whites. Under the Agricultural Adjustment Act (AAA) thousands of black farmers were forced to leave their land.

The Minimum Wage and Social Security Acts (page 43) were important changes introduced by Roosevelt, but they did not make life easier for most black people. They did not have equal opportunities in education or in employment. 65 per cent of black workers were employed as farm labourers or servants. These jobs were not protected in the New Deal laws, so most black people did not benefit. The New Deal protected unionised jobs – blacks were employed in few of these.

A Black people were often shown as servants or as simple-minded, childish people. Sometimes they were both, as in this 1939 film, *Gone With The Wind*.

Native Americans and the New Deal

Before the New Deal the Bureau of Indian Affairs controlled the activities of Native Americans. Most of their good land had been taken away from them. Instead they had been given small pieces of land and had been encouraged to become farmers and wear 'white people's' clothes. This of course was the opposite of the traditional way of life for the nomadic tribes who had followed the buffalo across the Plains.

John Collier was a social worker who in his job had got to know and respect Native Americans. He disapproved of the policy of trying to force Native Americans to copy white people's way of life. Roosevelt chose John Collier to be Commissioner of Indian affairs. In 1934 the Indian Reorganization Act made changes to government policy. Collier tried to give the Native Americans more control over their lives. Seven million acres of land were returned to the Native Americans. At first sight this might seem like a huge amount of land – but

C The photograph shows Harold Ickes, Secretary of the Interior, presenting the Constitution for Indian self-rule to two Flathead chiefs.

it was only a small fraction of the land the Native Americans wanted – and much of the land was of poor quality. The government spent more money on educational programmes on native American reservations. Jobs were provided for more Native Americans in the Indian Bureau. Tribes were encouraged to produce jewellery and blankets.

Collier worked hard but there were limits to what he could achieve. Native Americans still lived in great poverty in isolated communities with very poor facilities. Many of them were still very suspicious of Roosevelt's government. The constitution of 1935 was supposed to allow the Native Americans to rule themselves. It did not really give them the control they wanted and it did not give them back their traditional way of life. Native Americans still suffered from prejudice and discrimination.

B Native Americans or Red Indians were usually shown as blood-thirsty savages in Hollywood westerns.

Q

1 Look at sources A and B.
   a) If you only had these photographs to go on, what might you think black people and Native Americans were like?
   b) What are the problems in using Hollywood images, such as sources A and B, to find out about life for black people and Native Americans during the New Deal?

2 What evidence can you find to suggest that black people did not do well in the New Deal?

3 Compare the treatment of black people and Native Americans in the New Deal. Which group do you think did better in the New Deal? Why?

CONCLUSION – WINNERS AND LOSERS IN THE NEW DEAL?

Who gained from Social Security?

Roosevelt was very proud of the Social Security Act of 1935. He called it the greatest of the New Deal laws. Some of the ideas behind it are shown in source B. Each state would run its Social Security programme and decide how much should be paid out. The main part of the Social Security Act, however, was the creation of a pension fund for retired people over the age of 65. In 1937 employers and workers began paying in their contributions to set up a social security fund. By 1940 the fund was paying out small retirement pensions. Roosevelt said that the pension plan was not supposed by itself to provide a comfortable retirement. It was supposed to add to people's other sources of income. It was only later that many politicians and voters saw Social Security as the main source of retirement income.

Roosevelt knew that Americans didn't like paying taxes, but thought that people would be prepared to pay their Social Security contributions so that they could feel that they had earned their pensions. He said to one of his friends '…with those taxes in there, no damned politician can ever scrap my Social Security programme'.

Criticisms of the Social Security Act

- The old age pensions were very small – it was hard to live on a pension of $10 a month when the average monthly wage was $80.
- The Social Security Act helped the strong and well organised groups such as the trade unions, but other groups such as tenant farmers, unskilled labourers and domestic servants did not benefit.
- Native Americans, Mexican immigrants and black people suffered. The National Association for the Advancement of Colored People was an organisation which tried to win equal rights for black people. One of its officials said that Social Security 'looks like a sieve with the holes just large enough for the majority of Negroes to fall through'.

- Everyone paid in the same amount – whether they were rich or poor. Many saw this as unfair.
- Opponents of Social Security said that the money paid in by workers could have been used to get the economy going again – instead of being 'tied up'.
- The payments to disabled people were tiny – for example in 1937 a blind person only got $5 a week in New York City.
- Conservatives felt that it went too far – and they did not see why they should have to pay contributions.
- Liberals felt that it didn't go far enough – and that the payments should be bigger.
- Some Republican opponents of Roosevelt criticised the Social Security Act because they thought it was a threat to the traditional American way of life. They felt that the government should not interfere in the lives of the people by taking money away from workers for Social Security payments.

A A government poster about the Social Security Act, which began to provide Americans with some financial protection against unemployment, illness and old age.

Workers paid a small amount each week from their wages. The rest of the money came from their employers.

Workers received sickness benefit if they became too ill to work.

Workers received a pension when they became too old to work.

The aim was to give help where it was needed so blind people, handicapped children and many other needy groups would benefit.

B Some of the ideas behind Social Security.

C An American historian looks back on the impact of the New Deal:

The New Deal helped African Americans survive the Depression, but it never tried to put an end to racial injustice. Although the programmes served blacks as well as whites, in the South the weekly payments blacks received were much smaller … Overall, the New Deal provided assistance to 40 per cent of the nation's blacks during the Depression. Uneven as his record was, Roosevelt had still done more to aid this oppressed minority than any previous President since Lincoln. One African American newspaper commented that while 'relief and WPA are not ideal, they are better than the Hoover bread lines and they'll have to do until something real comes along' … Public service was one of the few professions open to women. A decade that was grim for most Americans was especially hard on American women … Above all, FDR had succeeded in establishing the principle of government responsibility for the old, the handicapped, and the unemployed.

Q

1 Look at source A.
a) What do you think was the aim of the poster?
b) What clues are there in the poster to explain why some people didn't benefit from Social Security?
2 Read the list of criticisms of Social Security. How would you defend Social Security? Make a list of good points about Social Security.
3 Look back at the section on Opposition to the New Deal (pages 44–47). Which of the criticisms of Social Security were also made about other New Deal laws?
4 'The New Deal helped African Americans survive the Depression, but it never tried to put an end to racial injustice' (source C). Discuss this interpretation, using the sources from this unit and your own knowledge.

ACTIVITY: WINNERS AND LOSERS IN THE NEW DEAL

Look at the illustrations. They tell you about how different people were affected by the New Deal. Some of them were real people, but the rest are based on real people and events that really happened.

1 FD Roosevelt

You won the election of 1932 and introduced many new laws to help relieve the suffering of the Depression and to get people back to work. There was a lot of opposition to your New Deal laws, but you beat your opponents and won the 1936 election. You did not solve all the economic and political problems you faced, but you managed to be re-elected President in the 1940 election. (For more information see pages 36–39 and 42–48.)

2 Frances Perkins

You are a supporter of Roosevelt's Democratic Party and have worked with FDR since 1910. Roosevelt gave you the important job of Secretary of State for Labor. You are the first woman ever to get a Cabinet minister's job. (For more information see pages 52–53.)

3 Bank Clerk

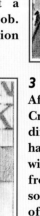

After the Wall Street Crash your bank ran into difficulties. Many people had lost their jobs and withdrew their savings from the bank. Roosevelt sorted out the bank crisis of 1933 (see page 40). Your bank survived as did your job.

4 A Tennessee Valley Authority farmer's wife

Before the New Deal you lived in poverty. Your land was eroded, your house had no electricity and your youngest child died of malaria. Since they built the dams your life has changed. The river is less polluted and the fields are more fertile. Experts have helped you to use new farming methods and grow more crops. You even have electricity in the house. Your eldest son is doing well – he has got a job at the new power station. (See pages 50–51.)

5 Ford car-worker

You moved to Detroit in 1914 and your wages of $5 a day made you one of the best paid car workers. The job is very boring, but you are doing better than millions of other Americans who lost their jobs in the Depression. You are worried that the factory might have to close because many people can't afford to buy cars. You have heard that workers in other car factories have been helped by the new trade unions to get better wages and working conditions. You are worried that people who go on strike might lose their jobs. (See pages 28–29.)

6 A Dust Bowl tenant farmer's wife from Oklahoma

You and your husband worked hard for many years to pay the rent on your small farm. The prices for your crops went down and the landowner forced you to leave your home. You had to pack up and drive to California. It has been hard to find work picking fruit. You are even poorer than you were in Oklahoma and you have no home. You did not get any money from the AAA or from Social Security. Men get first pick of the jobs. (See pages 48–49.)

The USA 1919–41 © Peter Mantin. Published by Hodder and Stoughton.

7 Henry Ford

You started building cars in 1896. Your Model T car brought cheap motoring to the masses and made you a huge fortune in the 1920s. You are worried about Roosevelt because you do not trust his New Deal. Roosevelt has allowed trade unions to be created, but you do not think workers should need trade unions. Roosevelt has not done enough to help the car industry recover from the Depression. Car manufacturers like you are still very rich, but have lost money because many people can no longer afford cars. (For more information see pages 28–29.)

8 A black hotel porter

Your family came from Mississippi, but you did not get much money working in the cotton fields. The racism was terrible. You saw a black man lynched – and the people who lynched him were not punished. You moved to New York in search of a better life. At first you had to live in a Hooverville, but finally you found a tiny apartment in Harlem. It was hard to get a job during the Depression, but eventually you found work as a hotel porter. The job is boring and you don't qualify for Social Security, but at least it is not as hard as farm work. White people are still racist towards you, but at least you are safer now. (See pages 10–15.)

9 Eleanor Roosevelt

You are married to the President. You supported him throughout his long illness and helped him when he was campaigning to be President. You did not just want to sit back and do nothing, so you have become involved in meeting ordinary Americans. You have travelled across the country finding out about the problems of poor Americans, blacks, whites, men and women. You would like to help people (pages 52–53).

10 A Native American woman, aged 60

In the 1920s your family moved away from the Reservation and went to the city. It was so different from your traditional way of life. You were looking for work but found that Native Americans were last in the queue when jobs were being given out. There was racial prejudice and poverty in the city. You moved back to the Reservation in 1935. You are still very poor. Thanks to Mr Collier's Indian Reorganization Act your daughter now has a teaching job on the Reservation. You are worried that your son will not find a job, and that you will not qualify for one of the new pensions. (See page 55.)

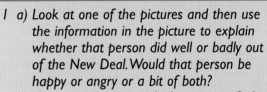

1 a) Look at one of the pictures and then use the information in the picture to explain whether that person did well or badly out of the New Deal. Would that person be happy or angry or a bit of both?
   b) You can get extra marks by trying to find out more about that person or group of people by looking back at other pages in the book.
2 Listen to what other people in the group say about their pictures. Think about who was doing well and who was doing badly out of the New Deal.
3 Cut up photocopies of the pictures and try to arrange them on your desk in a way which shows who you think were the winners and losers in the New Deal. Be ready to explain why you put the pictures in that order. Compare your results with those of other people.

Extended writing
Using all the pictures and information write an essay entitled: 'Who were the winners and who were the losers in the New Deal?'

The USA 1919–41 © Peter Mantin. Published by Hodder and Stoughton.

10

Why did the American Economy Recover?

What part did Roosevelt's New Deal play in the recovery of the economy? What part did the Second World War play in the recovery? Which was more important in the recovery, the New Deal or the Second World War?

Roosevelt's New Deal and the economic recovery

You might hear politicians talking about the economy, and about who should get the praise when things go well, or the blame when things go badly. If you look at source B you can see that the American economy seemed to be recovering from the Depression, but how would you decide when that recovery began and who should get the praise for it?

A New York taxi driver, interviewed on television in the 1960s, had no doubt about who had brought about the recovery. He said that Roosevelt was 'God in this country'. Roosevelt recognised the importance of staying in touch with the American people and spoke to them in his radio 'fireside chats' about the country's economic problems. Roosevelt used the fireside chats to tell the American people about the New Deal. Roosevelt explained that the Alphabet Laws were helping the economy recover because ordinary Americans were getting back to work. Roosevelt claimed that his policies had the support of most Americans. He told the nation about the huge numbers of letters from people who supported his attempts to beat the Depression.

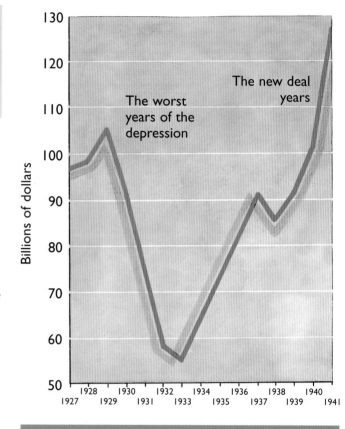

B This graph shows changes in the national income of the USA between 1927 and 1941. This is worked out by adding up the values of all the goods (cars, steel etc) and services (transport, catering etc) produced and the taxes collected by the government in one year (See page 33).

C A British school textbook writer looks back at the success of the New Deal (from *Roosevelt and the United States* by D B O'Callaghan, 1974).

Although few people realised it at the time, the main part of the New Deal was practically completed by 1938. Its most obvious achievement was that it had begun to bring the United States out of the Depression. Industrial workers, farmers, business men – people from almost every section of the community in fact – were better off in 1938 than they had been in the dark days of 1932. Most, though not all of them, gave the credit for this improvement to the New Deal. But the New Deal's achievement went further than this. By using the power of the Federal Government to ensure fairer treatment for the ordinary citizen, Roosevelt had given the American people renewed faith in their country and its way of life.

A One of the most famous letters President Roosevelt received was written by an ordinary worker in 1935 who had appealed to the President for help in his troubles. He wrote:

Dear Mr President,
    This is just to tell you everything is all right now. The man you sent found our house all right and we went down to the bank with him and the mortgage can go on for a while longer. You remember I wrote you about losing the furniture too. Well, your man got it back for us. I never heard of a President like you, Mr Roosevelt.

F An American newspaper cartoonist's view of the effects of Roosevelt's policies, January 1934. The cartoon is entitled 'The Sower'.

D An American history textbook weighs up the successes and failures of the New Deal (from *America: Past and Present*, 4th edition, by Divine, Fredrickson and Williams, 1995).

The New Deal lasted a brief five years. The least impressive achievement of the New Deal came in the economic realm. Whatever credit Roosevelt is given for relieving human suffering in the depths of the Depression must be balanced against his failure to achieve recovery in the 1930s. The moderate nature of his programmes, especially the NRA led to slow and halting industrial recovery. Although much of the advances that were made came as a result of government spending … the nation had barely reached the 1929 level of production a decade later, and there were still nearly ten million men and women unemployed.

E A British historian examines Roosevelt's achievements (from *The USA 1917–1980* by N Smith, 1996):

Unemployment was far lower by 1939 than it had been in 1932, and America survived the Depression without the threat of dictatorship which affected millions of people in Europe … Roosevelt extended government welfare that helped all groups, he worked with the trade unions, and the ordinary working man gained greater protection and increased wages. Social security, subsidies to farmers and most of all the idea that government could and should seek to assist people in times of hardship are an enduring legacy for America from the New Deal. A 1982 survey of 49 American historians ranked Roosevelt as the second greatest president out of 38 – Abraham Lincoln was in first place.

Q

1. a) Copy source B
   b) What can you tell from source B about the recovery of the economy?
2. According to source C, why was America able to recover from the Depression?
3. Source E suggests that the most important feature of the New Deal was that the government helped ordinary people when they faced poverty. Is this view closer to that of source C or D? Use quotations from the sources in your answer.
4. How might the author of source C use source B to back up what he writes about America's recovery from the Depression?
5. Do you think the person who drew the cartoon in source F was a supporter or an opponent of Roosevelt's New Deal? Mention things you see in the cartoon to support your answer.
6. Sources A and D give different interpretations of the New Deal. Using sources A to F and your own knowledge give reasons for this difference.

THE SECOND WORLD WAR AND ECONOMIC RECOVERY

Building the planes

When the USA joined the Second World War, President Roosevelt promised the Allies that he would supply 60 000 war planes a year. This was a huge promise to make when you remember that no country had ever made so many planes so quickly before, and that the USA didn't yet have a huge air-force. Goering, the Head of the German Air Force, said that it could not be done. He told Hitler that: 'The Americans cannot build airplanes. They are very good at refrigerators and razor blades.' He had heard about American production-line methods but did not think that they could be used to make so many planes and other weapons of war.

Factories were built with incredible speed. The production line methods were so successful that in one factory the materials came in at one end of the room and a finished plane came out an hour later at the other end. It then went straight onto the runway to be tested.

Many of the workers had no previous experience in building aircraft. Large numbers of women worked in the new factories while the men were away fighting in the armed forces.

> One of the biggest American aircraft factories was built in only six months on farmland near Detroit. The production line was so big that it was called 'the most enormous room in the history of man'. If you joined eight football pitches together they still wouldn't be big enough to fill the room.

The women proved that they could do the work just as well as the men.

In 1943 American factories produced 86 000 planes. Roosevelt's target of 60 000 had been smashed.

Building the ships

The Allies desperately needed ships to transport supplies of food and war materials. The problem needed to be solved quickly because German U-boats sank so many Allied ships. Roosevelt asked Henry Kaiser to build some of the new ships for him. This might have seemed a strange choice because Henry Kaiser had never built a ship before. Henry Kaiser liked nothing better than being told that a job was impossible – and then proving everybody wrong. He was told that his plans to build the Grand Coulee Dam were impossible – so he went ahead and built it. He was told that he knew nothing about shipbuilding – so he went ahead and built his new 'Liberty ships'. They weren't very pretty to look at, but Kaiser could build them in four days and he could build enough of them to keep the Allied war effort supplied.

Roosevelt thought that the way to win a modern war was to have far more of everything than your opponents. When the Americans won their battles in northern Europe against the Germans, they did not win by better strategy but by having more equipment. As one American put it: 'For America, war meant a mass production war. You design something on the production line, you lay it on and there it is.'

A A production line of Dauntless dive bombers at the Douglas factory, California. 5000 of these planes were produced in this factory.

B The historian Geoffrey Hodgson looks at the effects of the Second World War on the economic recovery of the USA (from *In Our Time*, 1976).

During Franklin Roosevelt's first term, the New Deal did not cure the underlying economic problems. It was the war that did that. Within a matter of months, six million workers found new jobs. Within a couple of years, mass unemployment had virtually disappeared. Soon the Great Depression itself was becoming an unhappy memory. The war boom brought record profits, with one third of all war orders to 10 giant firms. The war also meant an end to hard times for most of the population. Even allowing for inflation, real wages [the money people actually earned] jumped by 44 per cent in the four years of the war.

C Frances Perkins, writing in 1947, remembers the achievements of the New Deal. She had been Secretary of Labor in Roosevelt's government (from *The Roosevelt I Knew*, 1947).

The main reason for our economic recovery was the spending of government money on public works, work relief, and agricultural adjustment and resettlement programmes.

D A British historian looks at the reasons for the economic recovery (from *Franklin D Roosevelt* by Michael Simpson, 1989).

If the test of anti-Depression policies is the extent to which they reduce unemployment, then the New Deal rates five marks out of ten; almost eighteen million were jobless in 1933, and nine million were still unemployed in 1939. Moreover, at any given time, the New Deal assisted only a third of the workless, while as thousands of blacks, senior citizens and farmers could testify, the 'forgotten man' often remained forgotten. Other economic indicators recorded better gains, but the economy as a whole remained sluggish until rescued by war.

Why, at best, only two cheers for the New Deal? Part of the blame rests with Roosevelt. He made little attempt to tackle the roots of injustice and inequality. Nevertheless, the government was not completely to blame for the weaknesses of the New Deal. The destruction caused by the Great Depression was so complete that even if Roosevelt had struck the right path at once and stuck to it, almost certainly it would have taken at least eight years to repair.

Year	Estimated Unemployment
1929	1.55
1930	4.34
1931	8.02
1932	12.06
1933	12.83
1934	11.34
1935	10.61
1936	9.03
1937	7.70
1938	10.30
1939	9.48
1940	8.12
1941	5.56
1942	2.66
1943	1.07

E These figures show how many millions of people were unemployed in the USA, 1929–43.

1. Show the figures in source E as a graph or chart.
2. Using source E explain when you think the recovery began. Quote figures from source E.
3. How were the USA's economic problems cured? Compare the explanations in sources B and C.
4. Is the explanation of the economic recovery in source D nearer to that in source B or source C? Back up your answer with quotations.
5. Why do you think there are different points of view about whether the New Deal caused the economic recovery?
6. The New Deal Debate. Look back through the evidence in this unit (pages 60–63). Collect as much evidence as you can for:

- the view that the New Deal caused the recovery;
- the view that the Second World War caused the recovery;
- the view that the recovery was caused by both the New Deal and the Second World War.

See which 'side' wins.

Glossary

Allies – countries which fought alongside USA in the First World War (they included Britain, France, Russia and Italy)

Alphabet Laws – these laws were named after the initials of the agencies set up as a part of the New Deal

anarchists – people who wanted to destroy the capitalist system

capitalist – the opposite of a communist. Capitalists believe that businesses should be owned privately and not by the state

census – a population count

communist – a follower of the ideas of Karl Marx. Communists believe in a workers' revolution and a society in which wealth is shared equally

Congress – the law-making body, or parliament, of the USA. It has two parts, or 'houses' – the Senate and the House of Representatives

Constitution – the set of rules for the government of the USA, set out in the late 18th century. Changes to these rules are known as 'amendments' to the Constitution

democratic – a democratic country or democracy is a country which has regular elections, in which politicians have to be voted into power by the people

Democrat – a member of the Democratic Party. The Democratic Party is one of the two main American political parties. It has been seen as being more sympathetic to the problems of the poor and black Americans

Depression – the very serious economic crisis which hit the USA after the Wall Street Crash. Too many goods were produced, not enough people were prepared to buy, and millions lost their jobs. The Depression lasted throughout the 1930s

Dust Bowl – terrible dust storms hit large areas of farming land in which the soil was too dry and exhausted to produce crops. The farmers had to leave their land

federal – the USA is one nation, but made up of 50 states. This collection of states is a federation. Things which concern all of the states are 'federal'

flappers – usually richer American women who followed the new fashions of the 1920s and shocked their mothers with their carefree ideas

Governor – the top man or woman in the government of each state. He or she is elected by the voters of that state

House of Representatives – one of the two 'houses of parliament'. Representatives are elected to the House from each state. The House of Representatives raises money through taxes

hundred days – in the first hundred days of his presidency Roosevelt introduced many policies to try to get the economy going again

isolationism – the idea that the USA should not play an important part in European problems, but should be more concerned with what was happening at home

Jim Crow laws – local racist laws which treated black people as second-class citizens

League of Nations – an international organisation set up in 1919 as part of the Treaty of Versailles. It tried to solve international problems by discussion

lynching – taking the law into your own hands and hanging someone without waiting to find out whether a court of law found them guilty or innocent

New Deal – the name given to Roosevelt's economic recovery plan

President – the elected head of the American government

provenance – where a source comes from. Who wrote it? When? Who was intended to read it? What role did the writer have?

quota – placing strict limits on the numbers of people allowed to enter the USA. Some countries were allowed a bigger share or quota of immigrants than others

'Reds' – people with socialist or communist beliefs

republic – a country without a monarch. America used to be ruled by the British king, until 1776 when the Americans had a revolution and broke away from British control to become a republic

Republican Party – one of the two main political parties. Calvin Coolidge and Herbert Hoover were Republican presidents. The Republicans have been seen as being more sympathetic to the interests of wealthy Americans

Senate – one of the two 'houses of parliament'. Two people are elected from each American state to sit in the Senate. The agreement of the Senate is needed before a new law can be passed

sharecroppers – poor tenant farmers who worked on the land. Many of them suffered in the 1930s

Supreme Court – the most powerful court in the land. Its judges have the power to decide whether laws passed by Congress are legal or not

Uncle Sam – the symbol of the USA. He is seen as wearing clothes in the colours of the American flag

Vice-President – if the President is very ill, or dies in office, his assistant, the Vice-President takes over